Parent Talk!

The Art of Effective Communication
With the School and Your Child

Cheli Cerra, M.Ed. & Ruth Jacoby, Ed.D.

JOSSEY-BASS
A Wiley Imprint
www.josseybass.com

Published by Jossey-Bass
A Wiley Imprint
989 Market Street, San Francisco, CA 94103-1741 www.josseybass.com

Jossey-Bass books and products are available through most bookstores. To contact Jossey-Bass directly call our Customer Care Department within the U.S. at 800-956-7739, outside the U.S. at 317-572-3986 or fax 317-572-4002.

Jossey-Bass also publishes its books in a variety of electronic formats. Some content that appears in print may not be available in electronic books.

ISBN: 0-471-72013-5

Printed in the United States of America

10 9 8 7 6 5 4 3 2 1

The Buzz About Parent Talk!

"An absolute must read for every parent. The open lines of communication between a parent and teacher are essential and these authors show you exactly how to position your child for success."

Dr. G. L. Dempsey
Clinical Psychologist
Houston, TX

"Authors Cheli Cerra and Dr. Ruth Jacoby have done it! Parent Talk! is the must-have book for parents of school age children—kindergarten through high school! They have compiled 'Snapshots' of every conceivable situation that can arise between you, your child and your school. They offer easy-to-read, clear, simple suggestions on ways to deal with the situation AND include a Parent-to-Parent Tip!"

Margaret Wolter
President, ASTAR
Advocates for Students, Teachers, Administrators & Resources

"As a parent there are many times when we wished we could turn to a book that had all the answers we are looking for. Parent Talk! is just that book. An excellent book filled with practical advice and simply written insights to guide and support parents in our most important role, helping our children become the best that they can be."

Debbie Milam
Founder, *Creating Peace Project*
www.creatingpeaceproject.org

To our children, who provided us with the rich experiences of parenting.

Table of Contents

Table of Contents

How to Use This Book

Just like you, we are working parents. We know how busy you are, and the last thing we want this book to do is give you more work. What we do want is to empower you with the essential knowledge and effective actions you can take to make sure your child is achieving and show you what you can do with this knowledge when faced with a difficult situation within the school setting. This book gives you those tools, simply and quickly.

We have written this book to be easy to read. The snapshots you find throughout this book reflect real-life situations parents face in dealing with teachers and their own children. While the book follows the seasons, divided into quarterly topics, the information can be put to use year-round. The situations presented here are some we personally have experienced as parents, as well as scenarios we have experienced working with thousands of parents and children in our combined fifty-plus years in education. Each situation is followed by strategies and communication tips on how you can speak with your child, from elementary through high school. There are worksheets, checklists, charts, and sample letters to guide you. At the end of each chapter we have added role-playing suggestions, questions to ask your child or the school, and additional resources for further information. By utilizing these quick and simple tools, you will become confident, and that confidence will benefit both you and your child!

You will be:
- **Proactive:** Become a take-charge parent and a can-doer, working in your child's best interest;
- **Organized:** Keep all your communications to and from the school in a safe place, and consistently update a calendar of events the entire family can view;
- **A Good Record-Keeper:** Maintain all of your child's test scores, returned assignments, report cards, and progress reports in sequential order;
- **An Accurate Reporter:** Act as an informed contributor and document information at school conferences; and
- **An Advocate:** Be the greatest supporter of your child.

Because all of us are unique in our learning styles and the way we understand and process information, we have included different methods for learning. With the tips, scenarios, and worksheets presented in this book, we hope to shed light on and make simple the art of communication with your child and with your child's school personnel. When you are well prepared for an encounter, communication comes more easily and clearly for both the speaker and the listener, leading to solutions and possible compromises for any situation you need to address.

Your real-life situations may include elements of multiple snapshots. You can mix and match and adapt them to fit your comfort zone and individual circumstance. Throughout the book we have also added parent-to-parent tips. Use the tip information to guide you through each situation. The sample letters, worksheets, charts, keys, and tips should be used to assist you in communicating successfully with your child and his or her teacher. At the end of each chapter, you will be given a P. S. **"P"** stands for **"Practice and Role-play"**; **"S"** stands for **"Sample Script,"** which will help you understand and show you how to go through an actual role-play on the chapter's focus.

Before you begin, we recommend that, as your first step in your journey toward becoming an effective communicator, you take the **Communication Skills Assessment** *(Worksheet #1*, page 112*)*. This will help you determine your level of comfort when speaking with the teacher and your child, recognize your areas of strength, and target those areas where you need some assistance. We have also included a **Quarterly Self-Evaluation Checklist** *(Worksheet #2,* page 113*)* to keep you on track.

As you read and practice the tips throughout this book, you will learn how to establish a positive working relationship with teachers and ultimately help your child achieve success—not just in school, but in life.

Be open-minded to a teacher's suggestions.

Notes:
_____

_____

_____

_____

_____

_____

_____

_____

_____

_____

INTRODUCTION:
A Communication Blueprint for a Successful School Year

> "Education is not preparation for life; education is life itself."
> **John Dewey**

Congratulations! Being your child's greatest advocate and supporter also means being his representative, guiding and advising him as he faces each new school year and each challenge. After reading this book, you will be skillful and confident in presenting important points you want to communicate to your child's teacher. You will come across as an informed parent and your child's greatest advocate and supporter, whether in a face-to-face meeting, during a phone conference, in notes or letters to the school, or through Internet contact.

Be positive about education.

You are your child's representative throughout his life. As a representative you need to be sure that your child is getting the most appropriate and best education with all of the instructional advantages. You do not want your child to be left behind. You need to be kept apprised of your child's effort and academic progress and make sure that he gets every opportunity from the school to help him to succeed. To do this, you must maintain a sharp eye. Do not presume everything is fine. Become involved in your child's education. Ask questions. Talk to your child. Talk to your child's teacher. Don't be afraid to ask for help, or feel you are somehow inferior because you are not an expert. You are an expert. As a parent, you are the foremost expert on your child. You are the one most qualified to be his representative and biggest supporter. From the first day your child enrolls in school and throughout his entire school career, you must be his advocate. If you feel that your child needs extra help in school, ask for it. If you notice your child has trouble keeping up, say so. If you think your child is not being challenged in school, speak up. Communicate! Create a dialogue with the school. Create a team working for success.

In the following pages, you will find fifty-two snapshots that portray situations parents are likely to encounter with their child, the school, and the teachers.

Accompanying each snapshot will be strategies you can immediately put to use to direct the outcome of each situation so that your child, you the parent, and the teacher all benefit. As you practice these skills and become a better communicator, you will not only acquire a tremendous feeling of personal power, but also find teachers responding positively to your confidence and ability. By building on this bridge of cooperative communication, you will be able to help your child succeed in school and beyond.

Remember: You are the one who can make a difference. You are a parent!

Parent-to-Parent Tip:

One of the greatest things a parent can do for a child is to communicate with that child from day one. From birth through childhood, from those difficult teenage years to adulthood, you want your child to talk to you. And when he does, it is important for you to listen.

You have many opportunities to get to know your child through various sources. One of them is to volunteer at your child's school. Being in your child's school will give you insights you can't get anywhere else. Get to know your child's friends. They will open another window into your child's personality. Create a dialogue with your child's teachers and coaches. They want your child to succeed and can give you valuable information on how to help your child do so.

Many parents start off being very involved at the elementary school level, then taper off as their kids become older, more independent, and able to do many things for themselves. Yet, children need their parents' involvement at every level of their education—especially during the middle and high school years, where parents must compete with their child's peers, cultural trends, attractive advertising, and other influences in forming their child's values. Even though you encourage independence in your child, he still needs your input and guidance. You want to be there for him and know he feels confident in discussing with you whatever troubles him.

Think back to the time your mother had to handle a difficult situation you put her into when you were a child. How did she handle it? Did her techniques work and, if so, which ones? Try and figure out what your mother did to help solve the problem without destroying your confidence. Focus on the successful methods she used.

Role-play is a great way for children—and adults—to learn how to solve problems. Modeling and practicing can make a difficult situation easier to handle. You can use role-play to process thoughts and ideas so that you and your child can communicate them in a constructive and positive way.

Stage all of your snapshots and concerns prior to school meetings and before confronting your child. When you have planned and practiced what you want and need to say, you will have the advantage of feeling relaxed and comfortable during the actual meeting, allowing you to ease the tension of a tough situation. **Remember, role-play, praise, and practice.**

HOW TO ROLE-PLAY

1. Be calm.

2. Choose a quiet area.

3. Set aside 30 minutes.

4. Be ready to learn from and listen to each other.

As an effective communicator, I will be…

Proactive: Speaking out as an advocate for my child in his school.

Organized: Keeping my child organized so that his schoolwork and classwork are ready every day. Logging upcoming tests and reports on a calendar and updating my child's planners daily. These help my child—as well as me—stay on top of all assignments and school events throughout the year.

Willing Participant: Joining the parent organization of the school and attending as many meetings as possible. I will be ready to listen, guide, advocate, and support my child and his school.

Effective: Listening attentively, giving equal time to all sides, and creating solutions for success will be a primary goal with my child at home and in school. I will be well prepared to compromise with my child and the teachers and work together in assisting my child to succeed.

Resourceful: Recognizing and knowing where to find the school's and school district's rules and regulations, as well as any other pertinent information I may need to help my child succeed.

In doing this I will have the P.O.W.E.R.!

Notes: _____

_____

_____

_____

_____

_____

_____

_____

_____

_____

SECTION ONE: SUMMER
Gearing Up for School Success

"I like a teacher who gives you something to take home to think about besides homework."
Lily Tomlin as "Edith Ann"

Snapshot #1:

My Child Has the Back-to-School Blues

www.school-talk.com

Parent-to-Parent Tip:

For a successful start to the school year, bring **Getting to Know My Child** (*Worksheet #5, page 116*) to your first parent-teacher conference.

My child is starting a new school and is very concerned about the new school year. He is anxious about making new friends, meeting new teachers, and not knowing the school building or the neighborhood and its surroundings. To tell the truth, I am anxious too. What should I do?

Tip :

Elementary/Middle/High:

Call the school before the first day to find out if and when it is open. If it is, pay the school a visit. See if you and your child can meet the new teachers before school starts and tour the building to become more comfortable with it. You may want to call beforehand to make sure that the principal or other school personnel will be available to assist you. It's a good idea to start at the main office and sign in as a school visitor before walking around campus. If the principal is there, introduce yourself—smile and be friendly. If your child has any special needs for learning, is gifted, or requires any unusual accommodations, locate the school counselor, administrator, or specialist in that area and set up an appointment so you know your child's needs will be met immediately. Make sure that all your medical records and phone contact numbers are up-to-date and correct. Ask about his class schedule and when you can get a copy. Visit the school's website to get the school supply list for each teacher, if available, as well as other important information about the school. About a week before school starts, ease your child out of the casual summer vacation time schedule and into the school bedtime and morning routines. By getting used to the change in the time schedule before school starts, your child will be eager, ready, and less stressed when it's time to go—and so will you.

> **Be prepared for the new school year well ahead of the actual starting date. Being prepared will give your child greater security and confidence.**

Tip : **Extra Tip for Older Children:** Talk to your child about taking on the responsibility of getting prepared for school. Show your child how to set the alarm clock for the new hours and advise him to begin the schedule for getting up and going to bed a week before school begins to better understand what is expected. Even when your child takes responsibility for getting ready for the school year, however, you still need to check that everything is in order. If you let him know how proud you are for taking on that job and following through, he will start the year with the right attitude and will be well prepared. Remember, you are the parent and your input and guidance are still extremely important.

Parent-to-Parent Tip: Take your child for a practice ride or walk prior to the first day of school. Show your child the safest route to school. Create a safe haven if an emergency occurs. Talk about what to do and where to be if stormy weather occurs. Find out when and where there is adult supervision before and after school hours in case you decide to change the method your child uses for transportation. You may want to schedule a meeting with the teacher during the first week of school for him to get to know you and your child. Bring along **Getting to Know My Child** (*Worksheet #5*, page 116).

Getting Ready for School Checklist:

ITEM	YES	NO	ADDITIONAL
Uniform/school clothes			
Shoes/accessories			
School supplies			
Backpack/purse/lunchbox			
Extra school supplies for home			
School tour			
School orientation visit			
School schedule			
Updated medical records			
New health problems reported			
Correct emergency information			

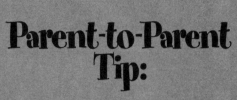

Parent-to-Parent Tip:

Shop with your elementary student for school supplies! Let him help make the choices on folders, notebooks, and other supplies. For older children, give them the responsibility for buying what's needed, but be sure to check their purchases and give the final okay. Buy extra supplies for home, such as glue, loose-leaf paper, markers, pen, pencils, and erasers. Back-to-school sale prices are usually excellent and supplies are readily available. Later in the year, not only will the prices be higher, it may not be as easy to find what you need.

Keep extra school supplies on hand so you won't have to go shopping at the last minute when your child runs out.

Snapshot #2:

I Am Recently Divorced and Have Sole Custody of My Child

I recently got divorced and received sole custody of my child. My ex-husband moved out of state and I have not seen him since the divorce. I recently heard he is back in town. I am afraid that he will try to take my child from school. Worse yet, he has threatened to do this. What should I do?

Tip:

Elementary/Middle/High:
Before the first day of school, call the school and make an appointment with the principal. At the meeting bring the official court document that says that you have sole custody of your child. Make sure that you give the principal all of your emergency contact numbers. The official school emergency information card will always have a place where you put who is allowed to take your child during the school day in case of emergency or illness. This person will have to show a picture identification before the child will be released. By letting the principal know of your situation, she will be able to alert the teachers and the school staff, as well as flag your child's records. When filling out the official school information card, make sure you put in bold letters that your child's father is NOT allowed to see or take your child. Once again, the school principal should have a system with the front office and the teachers to keep the child safe when situations such as these occur.

Parent-to-Parent Tip:

If you are separated, estranged, or divorced, you want to avoid having the school become involved in personal family conflicts. In many cases, the court specifies in the official court document which parent has custody of the child. If you have joint/shared custody, the document will state the adult who is the residential parent and who is the custodial parent. The residential parent is the parent whom the child lives with. In many cases, this is the parent who registers the child in school and fills out the necessary emergency information. Always present official court documents and communicate in person with the school principal when dealing with sensitive issues. Always keep your child's welfare uppermost in your thoughts and actions.

Snapshot #3:

My Child Does Not Speak English

W e just moved to the United States from South America. My son is having a hard time learning the English language. My husband and I are concerned that we will have difficulty communicating with the school. What should I do?

Parent-to-Parent Tip:

Get to know your child's guidance counselor; he can serve not only as a liaison between you, your child, and other school personnel, but can also assist your child with the adjustment issues he will most likely be facing. Ask if the school district has a program for adults to learn English. Learning English with your child can be a very positive experience. It will show your child that you value learning and education. Learning is a lifelong experience.

Get a list of the names and contact numbers of all key personnel at the school.

Tip :

Elementary/Middle/High:

When you visit the school, ask a person who speaks both your language and English to accompany you and act as your interpreter. Have your interpreter take notes in your native language on the important points of your meeting so you can have this information handy at any time. At the school, ask which staff members you should see when you need help with certain problems, such as: academic assistance for your child, bus schedules, medical information, and notices to be translated. Explain that you want to support your child and the school, but until you learn to communicate on your own, you would like to get as much help as possible. Use **Who's Who at the School** (*Worksheet #3*, page 114) to assist you. Ask what services are available to both of you. Repeat everything to make sure the interpreter relayed all of your concerns. Ask for a contact person at the school and introduce yourself so you will feel comfortable calling her with your questions. Have your child attend the conference with you so he understands that there are people at the school to whom he can go when he needs help. Set up a time when he can meet all of the school personnel who can assist him. This is important so he will know where and when to find them. You may want to ask if there is a student from the same country at the school who may be able to be your child's buddy until your son gets more proficient in English. They may become good friends as well.

24

Snapshot #4:

My Child's Friend Is a Bad Influence

Tip :

Teach your child to be responsible for her own behavior and its consequences.

My daughter made friends with another classmate last year who became a bad influence. My daughter had always been a good student and had never gotten into trouble. By the end of the school year, she had failed a class and had been in the principal's office several times. Problems occurred not only in school, but also after school when she got together with this girl. I do not want her having any contact with this child and am concerned that they will again be in class together. What should I do?

Elementary Middle/High:

Before school starts, make an appointment with the principal or assistant principal and talk about your concerns. Ask that your daughter not be placed in the same class/classes as this child. At this meeting you should give an example of an actual incident that happened with your daughter last year that made you come to this decision. This will help explain your position. If necessary, ask the administrator to pull up your daughter's behavior records and final grades as documentation of the problem. Be polite, but firm, as you insist that it's essential that she not be in the same classroom. Even if the school staff does make the necessary changes, continue to monitor her. Work with the school counselor and set up some clear boundaries at home. A good suggestion is to have your daughter sign a behavior contract with you stressing the outcomes you would like to see happen. Use the **Behavior Contract** on page 72. Prepare the contract with the school counselor and present it as a team effort. Make sure to establish clear consequences if any of the rules are broken. Explain to your daughter what you are doing and why. Make it clear that you feel this is necessary even though she may not agree. You, as the parent, have not only the right but the responsibility to make this decision. Talk to her about developing other friendships and learning better decision-making skills. You also need to discuss the importance of not forming negative habits and behaviors, regardless of what others may be doing. Express the fact that she alone is responsible for her behavior and its positive or negative consequences in her life. You may also want to establish a relationship with the school counselor who can give you resources and assistance for further help with your child. Parents also need to take responsibility in working with the school and setting boundaries with their children. Bad habits and behaviors left unchecked can have serious, long-lasting results.

Snapshot #5:

My Child Is Gifted and I Want Her Placed in the Gifted Program

www.school-talk.com

My child has always received A's and schoolwork seems to be extremely easy for her. The teacher agrees with me. I need to make sure the school places her in a class that will challenge her. What should I do?

Tip :

Elementary:
Once school begins, set up a conference with the teacher. Explain that you understand from comments on all of her school papers and report cards that your child is doing extremely well, and that all test scores show she is ahead of her grade level in reading and math. Bring in the previous two years' report cards to show the consistency of this trend. Ask the teacher what services the school provides for the children who are consistently ahead of their class. If there is a gifted program, ask what you can do to get her tested for placement. Talk to your child and make sure she is comfortable with a new classroom and placement. Many children may do well when allowed to go at their own pace, yet become stressed and perform below their ability when pushed to do more. Ask also whether the school's gifted program will take children away from the regular classroom part-time, and make sure your child is not penalized for the work she misses while participating in the gifted program, if that is the case.

> # A good-quality education program is geared to meet all students' needs.

Tip : **Middle/High:**
Once school begins, speak with the team of teachers your child has and ask how they view your child's academic ability. If they all agree that your child excels in academics, ask how you go about testing her for placement in more advanced classes or the gifted program. Ask about the program and the process for evaluating your daughter. Become informed on your child's rights for being tested in a timely fashion. Talk to your child and make sure she feels comfortable going into an honors course or Advanced Placement classroom. Ask the school counselor or administrator about "dual enrollment" type programs, which allow your child to attend high school and college at the same time. This can give your child confidence, knowing she can succeed at that level, but make sure that your child is emotionally ready. You do not want to add unnecessary stress and pressure.

Parent-to-Parent Tip:
Seek assistance. Recognize that your child has certain talents. Capitalize on her interests and create an environment enriched with materials that will challenge her and encourage exploration. You may need to increase your knowledge in those areas where your child shows an interest. Learn together and search out people and places that will increase your child's capabilities and learning enthusiasm. Recognize that your child learns at her own pace. Some children excel when given greater challenges; others do not.

Snapshot #6:

My Child Is Failing at a High-Performing School

We specifically moved to a new neighborhood last year with the best school in the area. This school has won many national awards of distinction and had the highest test scores in the state last year. However, my child did not do well and received two F's on his report card. With the new school year about to begin, I am concerned he is falling behind. What should I do?

Parent-to-Parent Tip:

Even though the school that your child attends may be rated high academically, it is extremely important that you monitor your child individually and not assume that he will be successful. A school's high academic rating does not necessarily translate into your child succeeding. Advocate on his behalf. Ask what is being done to help your child become successful. No matter what your child's level is, even if he is in special education classes or has Limited English Proficiency, make sure he is making adequate yearly progress. This means that he is steadily learning, improving, and moving forward in his educational experience.

Tip :

Elementary/Middle/High:
Make an appointment to meet with the principal before the first day of school. Bring your child's report card. Talk to the principal about your concerns and ask what standardized test your child was given and ask to see your child's scores. Have the principal explain the standardized test scores to you. Compare the scores to his report card and other tests, assignments, and projects. Find out if your child is reading on grade level. After you collect all of this information, create a plan with the principal. Set up a timeline where you will once again meet to discuss your child's progress. Use the **Assessment Tracker** on page 29 to keep this information handy. Find out the school district's policy in relationship to standardized testing. Some states use this information to promote children from one grade to the next and even for high school graduation.

Your child's progress, not the school's ranking or rating, must be your primary concern.

The Assessment Tracker

Is your child making the grade or falling behind? Tracking your child's report card grades and standardized tests from year to year will give you a better picture of how your child is learning and succeeding in school. Use the chart below to keep track of your child's progress.

Student Name:

Directions: Using the school records, fill in the student's standardized test scores. This is a recommended resource that you may want to keep in order to track the student's history on previous standardized tests. A history can provide a wealth of information for conferences, determining skill level, and seeking knowledge on a child's performance record. This is an easy snapshot of a child's test history.

	Math Level	Reading Level	Writing Level	ESL/LEP Level	IEP Status	Other	Teacher
K							
1st							
2nd							
3rd							
4th							
5th							
6th							

Snapshot #7:
My Child's Health Needs to Be Monitored and He Must Take Medication Daily

**W**hen my child complained of having difficulty breathing at school, I took him to the doctor, who diagnosed him with asthma. Now he has to take medication in the middle of the day while at school. Frankly, I'm worried. What if he has an asthma attack at school? What should I do?

Tip :

Elementary/Middle/High:

Notify the school and his teacher about your child's condition. Put it in writing and give a copy to everyone who works with your child. This is very important, as the school can flag your child as having a medical condition. Make sure that all medical forms and parent contact information are up to date in your child's records. You may want to call the school counselor, since some schools have programs to help children manage asthma. Ask for and fill out the appropriate medical form giving permission to a trained staff person or school nurse to administer the medication to your child during the school day. Make sure you have provided the medication to the appropriate school official for safe storage. Have the person in charge of the medication contact you when the supply begins to get low. Talk to your child about this plan. Make sure he understands that if he does not feel well, he should go to the office. Impress upon him that he must be responsible for how his body is feeling and to speak up right away if he can't breathe.

> *Make sure you have provided the medication to the appropriate school official for safe storage and that your child knows the location of the office and whom to see for medication when an attack occurs.*

Parent-to-Parent Tip:

Catching an asthma attack at an early stage can make a big difference in reducing its severity. You may want to go to the school and talk with the administration about the procedures they follow when an attack occurs. Bring in informative brochures for the staff to keep. Insist that you be called the minute your child has an attack. Make sure that all appropriate school officials know about your child's medical condition and that all emergency contact numbers are kept current. Your child's comfort in knowing that procedures are in place will remove much unnecessary anxiety, which some doctors believe contribute to some asthma attacks.

Snapshot #8:

My Child Has Diabetes

Tip:

Elementary/Middle/High:
Before the first day of school, call and make an appointment to see the school principal. At this meeting bring a letter informing everyone at the school who comes into contact with your child about her condition. Share with them the routines for medications, the possible signs of trouble, and under what circumstances your child should be allowed to go to the office. The school staff needs to know what to do in case of an emergency. Make sure that they have your best telephone contact number, and that they know to call you the minute your child does not feel well. Tell them how to handle any situation, and ask the teacher to allow your child to go to the office and have a snack when necessary. Practice with your child what the proper procedures are and when and how to follow them.

My child was diagnosed with diabetes three years ago. At her previous school, I had problems. Several times, when she felt ill, the homeroom teacher wouldn't let her go to the office. Many times after recess, the teacher would not allow my child to have a snack if she felt that she needed it. Because of my child's condition, certain procedures must be followed; otherwise, she may become ill or worse. What should I do?

> *Inform the school of all medical conditions and how they must be treated. Bring medical information and brochures if you have them.*

Parent-to-Parent Tip:

Make sure that your child knows the physiological signs that necessitate some food or medicine. Have your child keep an appropriate snack in his or her backpack. Ask the school about special programs. Many districts now have training workshops for school personnel that provide information on diabetes. Call the school district to see if such training exists, and if it does, request that someone from your child's school attend that workshop. Also, check with the school and the local school board about their policies on diabetic children, and make sure you and the school are following the correct procedures.

Snapshot #9:

I Just Moved to a New Community: How Do I Find a School for My Child?

We just moved to a new community and school starts in less than three weeks. I have not had any time to get my son registered in school. In fact, I don't even know what school to send him to. What should I do?

Tip : **Elementary/Middle/High:**
First, determine your options. Call the local school district or go on the Internet to find what school choices are available in your area. One of the better resources on the web is GreatSchools.net. Get the addresses of the schools in your area and visit each one, even if they aren't opened yet, just to have a look at the facility and the neighborhood. Second, after you have done some research and decided which schools will benefit your child, you can either call or go in person to find out the admission and registration procedures. Third, take a school tour with your child and ask questions. Following are the top ten questions to ask, depending on the age, grade, and special needs of your child.

Places to find information on schools:

1. GreatSchools.net
   http://www.GreatSchools.net
   An online guide to K-12 schools

2. Your local Chamber of Commerce

3. Your Realtor

Top Ten Questions to Ask When Visiting a School

Elementary:

1. What curriculum does the school use to foster school success?

2. What standardized tests does the school give students yearly? How does the school measure up? Is passing the tests a requirement for promotion?

3. How is student achievement measured? Is there assistance for children who need extra help?

4. Does the school have a safety plan?

5. Does the school have a discipline plan?

6. Does the school have an active parent organization? How can I join?

7. Does the school have extracurricular activities, clubs, and sports programs?

8. Does the school have a parent/student handbook?

9. Are there before- and after-school child-care programs?

10. What are the drop-off and pickup procedures?

Middle/High:

1. What curriculum does the school use to foster school success?

2. What standardized tests does the school give students yearly? How does the school measure up? Is passing the tests a requirement for graduation from high school?

3. How is student achievement measured? Is there assistance for children who need extra help?

4. Are Advanced Placement and honors courses provided?

5. Does the school have a safety plan?

6. Does the school have a discipline plan?

7. Does the school have an active parent organization? How can I join?

8. Does the school have extracurricular activities, clubs, and sports programs?

9. Does the school have a parent/student handbook?

10. Does the school have counselors who can help students get information and guide them in decisions on career goals, college placement, and other issues?

Snapshot #10:

My Child Does Not Want to Wear the School Uniform

I have decided to send my child to a school that mandates wearing uniforms, because I believe this will foster better discipline and a higher-quality education. My daughter is not happy about this decision. What should I do?

Tip :

Elementary:
Have a discussion with your child about your reasons for this decision. Offer to let her help pick out the uniform style and colors if there are options, perhaps letting her decide what to mix and match. Even though your child will not like your decision, it is yours to make.

Middle/High:
Again, discuss the rationale behind your choice with your child. Listen to your child's reasons, try to understand them, and then explain to her that you bear the responsibility for her education and you feel this choice is best. Perhaps you can say you'd be willing to compromise on other issues, like curfew, phone privileges, and makeup, but education comes first and this was the school of your choice. Tell her that if she does well now, when it comes time to choose a college, you will visit schools with her and make a decision on that together.

Parent-to-Parent Tip:

Talk to your child about your decision. Be sure to be specific and open for discussion. Your reasons should be logical and truthful. If purchasing the uniform places a financial burden on you, check with the school administration. They may have a program to assist you.

You are the parent; some decisions are yours to make.

34

P.S.: Practice *What to Say* When They Say...

> *"I don't care what you say, I still want to be friends with her and remain in the same class. You are not being fair."*

> *"My teacher is always ignoring me, she never listens to me. I hate her."*

"No one likes to be told who their friends should be, so I understand why you are angry with me. However, you have been getting into trouble since you have become friendly with this girl. This is unacceptable. Up until you developed this friendship, school had always been the most important part of your life. You behaved appropriately and worked hard to earn good grades. I would like to see you regain that positive and productive attitude."

"Let's decide on a time to discuss this further when neither one of us is distressed or angry. Maybe together we can come up with a suitable solution that is satisfying to both of us."

"Let's practice what to say to your teacher so that she knows that you have an important question or concern."

"No one likes to be ignored, so I understand why you are angry with your teacher. However, there are times that are best to ask for help. Let's go early to school tomorrow and talk to the teacher before school starts. You need to go up to her and say, Mrs. Smith, I need your help. Would you please help me with (state the problem or concern)? If the teacher tells you that she is busy, then ask her when would be a good time to talk: after school, during lunch, or before reading time."

"I would like to see you speak up for yourself when you have a question or a problem, but remember, you have to do it the right way. The right way is to be polite, state your problem or concern, and listen to what the teacher has to say."

35

SECTION TWO:
FALL
Parent Involvement Increases Student Achievement

"Too often we give children answers to remember rather than problems to solve."
John Dewey

Snapshot #11:
I Can't Attend Open House

My child brought home a notice saying Open House at his school would be held one evening next week. Since I work evenings, I asked for a different shift at work, but the manager wouldn't allow it. Both my child and I were disappointed. I had particularly wanted to meet the teacher and see how she is going to give assignments, grade papers, and talk about her philosophy of education. What should I do?

Keep in touch with the school—check the website.

My child's school website is:

_____

Participate in as many school events as possible. Call the school or go on the school's website to get a schedule. Give your employer as much advance notice as possible when requesting time off for school-related business.

Tip :

Elementary/Middle/High:
Ask for a calendar of school events as well as the Open House date well in advance so you will have as long as possible to make other arrangements. Try to obtain the manager's approval by offering to take vacation time or switch shifts with a co-worker. If you still cannot attend, call the teacher and explain your work circumstances. Ask for any handouts she may be giving out that night and for any papers that would help explain her grading policy, class rules, homework schedules, and other important information. Request that she get the phone number of and permission for you to call a parent who does attend, then phone that parent and talk about the Open House. Inform the teacher you would like to meet with her as soon as it is convenient for her to discuss her philosophy and policies. Ask for a team meeting (a meeting with all of your child's teachers), if possible, so you can get the answers to all your questions. Where teacher teams don't exist, contact or schedule a meeting with each individual teacher. Your child will know you are well informed on the school and classroom policies and your child's teacher will know that you are a concerned parent.

Snapshot #12:

My Child's School Has Mildew

Tip :

Elementary/Middle/High:
Contact the administration as soon as possible and set up a meeting to express your concern. Your child and the entire class may have to be taught in another room that is mildew-free until this problem is fixed. However, if your child has a medical condition which may be aggravated by such conditions as mold, mildew, carpet lice, poor ventilation, or air conditioning, let it be known immediately. Inform the principal that you would prefer not to have your child and his class moved, but you must put his health first. While this is a short-term resolution, it should be acceptable until the room is repaired.

I noticed in my child's classroom that a ceiling tile and a wall near the window had mildew. When I spoke to the teacher about it, she said she had put in a work order for the custodial engineer to fix the problem, but nothing had been done yet. I told her my child has allergies and this could aggravate his condition. What should I do?

> **Notify the school immediately when there is a safety issue at your child's school.**

Parent-to-Parent Tip:

Exploring the short-range accommodations for your child's health and the long-range solutions for the school should be a constructive and realistic dialogue.

Snapshot #13:
The School Is Always Doing Fundraisers

I resent having to participate in the school's constant fundraising. I feel I pay enough taxes for my child to get a good education. Every time I turn around, the school is either asking for money or making our kids go out and sell something to raise money. I feel like I never see any benefits from the fundraising anyway. What should I do?

Parent-to-Parent Tip:

Every school has a list of unmet needs for the year. Many teachers and school staff call this their "wish list." It could be art supplies, additional computers, or adult volunteers to tutor, help in the cafeteria during lunch, or after-school dismissal. Fundraising projects on the part of the parents and students can channel positive energy to contribute to the building of school spirit while, at the same time, improving the school.

Tip :

Elementary/Middle/High:
Speak to the principal or school administrator in charge of the fundraising project. Ask how the funds raised are being used. If this fundraising event is sponsored by the parent organization, have the parent leaders explain, at the next parent meeting, what the goals for the fundraisers are, and how that will benefit the school as a whole rather than each child individually. You may even have some suggestions on how to raise money. For example, perhaps you know a store or business that would donate items or money, or you might want to organize a schoolwide garage sale or auction. The main goal is to assist in making the school more unified and to give the students a high-quality education that can't be measured in a line-item budget. If you want to contribute to the fundraising, you can donate your time, which is just as important.

> ## *Be part of the solution, not part of the problem.*

Snapshot #14:

My Child Came Home Without Eating Lunch

My child came home from school today hungry and upset that the cafeteria manager would not allow him to eat lunch because she said I hadn't paid. Instead, they offered him cereal and milk. I signed my child up for the free or reduced lunch program last year and was told that it would continue this year. I am a single parent and cannot afford to give him money every day to eat lunch at school. I just started a new job and I cannot take time off to go to school to solve this problem. What should I do?

Tip:

Elementary:

Many schools provide peanut butter and jelly sandwiches or cereal and milk for those children who forget to bring either a lunch from home or money to buy lunch. Send a note to the teacher letting her know exactly what happened and ask her to follow up with the cafeteria manager. Reassure your child that he is on the school lunch program, but that a mistake was made. Let him know he needs to tell the teacher he did not get a regular lunch yesterday. Role-play the exact words for your child to say. Example: "Mrs. Davis, the cafeteria manager, would not give me lunch yesterday because she said I had not paid. My mom says I am on the school lunch program. She wrote you a letter about it." Send along a note or letter he can give to the teacher to explain the situation further.

Middle/High:

Let your child know that a mistake was made and he is still on the school lunch program. Have him go to the main office the very next morning and ask to speak to the counselor or assistant principal to explain the situation. Sending a note or letter from you will help his confidence and clear up any questions the school administration may have. Include your phone numbers where a school official can call you.

Parent-to-Parent Tip:

Breakfast and lunch programs provided by the federal government require that certain forms be completed by the parents, making sure that all information is correct. Returning the forms to the school on time can avoid any embarrassment your child might experience by being singled out in a cafeteria line. Many times the information on these forms must be updated and you must assist the school in keeping the records current.

41

Snapshot #15:

Why Should I Have to Volunteer in Another Classroom?

I want to volunteer in my child's classroom instead of in the main office. When I mentioned this to the teacher, she seemed very hesitant and acted like she didn't know what to say. I felt like she didn't want me around and now I'm wondering whether she may be hiding something. What should I do?

Tip :

Elementary:

Ask for a meeting with the teacher so you can find out why she was not as cooperative as you thought she should be. There could be any number of reasons why you aren't volunteering in your child's class. Perhaps there is paperwork you need to fill out, such as a volunteer form that requires information for a background check. You may have to attend a volunteer workshop to learn the rules and responsibilities of volunteers before you can enter any room and be in direct contact with students. It's even possible that your child's school does not allow a parent to work in the same class as his or her child.

Middle/High:

Rethink your position. Many older kids and young adults don't want their parent in their classroom or in a friend's room. You may volunteer to assist with the math club after school or to help in the office. All volunteering is important and appreciated. Ask your child what she is comfortable with before you commit yourself. If you decide not to work in the classroom at all, going to meetings of the school's parent organization and helping with special activities are other ways to get involved at this age level.

Parent-to-Parent Tip:

When you work full-time you can still help out at your child's school. For ideas, see **30 Ways to Help Out Your Child's School When You Work Full-Time** (*Worksheet #4*, page 115).

How to Be a Great Volunteer:

1. Tell the teacher in writing when you can volunteer, what you like to do, and how often you can come in.
2. Let the teacher know when you can't make it in.
3. Give the teacher all of your contact information.
4. Always go to the main office and sign in.
5. Remember, you are in the room to assist the teacher, not to enforce discipline.

How to Volunteer if You Are a Working Parent:

1. Read all notices to see if the teacher needs supplies.
2. If you have a day off, let the teacher know in advance so she can arrange for you to help out.
3. Volunteer to help make phone calls.
4. Collect items the teacher may need for art projects like magazines, recyclable goods, yarn, and empty containers.

"Involvement Challenge" A Personalized School Involvement Worksheet:

What's holding YOU back from getting involved in your child's school?

Finish the following sentences. I want to get more involved, but . . .

1. _____
2. _____
3. _____

Source: www.eduville.com

> *Volunteering can be very rewarding and extremely helpful to the school. Know school policies and the reasons behind them.*

Parent-to-Parent Tip:

Many schools have policies that do not allow parents to work as a volunteer in their children's classroom. If you have a particular skill—for example, a background in math—you could suggest that the school use your talents to run a math group. All children need caring and skilled adults to assist them. Think of the rewards you will receive when a child masters a skill you have taught. You may want to reconsider and still volunteer your time, even if it's with another teacher, in the main office, school cafeteria, or school library. Take the **Involvement Challenge** on pages 43–44 and challenge yourself to become involved. By giving of your time, you will have made a difference in a child's life and in your own.

Once you have identified what is holding you back, take a look at what you can do to change that. I can . . .

1. Participate more in school functions. Being there for my child is more important than the things on my to-do list.
2. Talk to my child's teacher to find out little things I can provide for his/her class.
3. Look around our home to see if I can find things that the school can really use, such as old magazines, extra pens and pencils, old books, and art supplies such as scissors, crayons, and markers.
4. Look in my calendar to see if I can contribute a little bit of my time in volunteering at my child's school or in the classroom.
5. Talk to my neighborhood's businesses to see if they have some supplies they can contribute for our school's functions and events.
6. Get excited about the school's upcoming social events and try to think about how I can help.
7. Volunteer during my child's lunchtime by monitoring the school's campus for safety.

"Involvement Challenge" Goal-Setting Your Involvement:

Write down a goal that you want to achieve in your child's school.
I plan to: _____

EXPECTATIONS
What will happen if you cannot meet your involvement challenge goal? Will you be disappointed or will you try to rework the goal?

ACTION
List three things that you can do to get involved.
1._____
2._____
3._____

Your "Involvement Challenge" Action Plan:

I will _____
By _____ **Date** _____
Date Completed _____
Signed: _____

Source: www.eduville.com

Snapshot #16:

My Child Does Not Have Textbooks

Tip :

Elementary/Middle/High:
First, meet with the teacher; let him know your concerns, and ask him when the textbooks will be arriving. If the teacher gives you an indication that he, too, has been waiting, make an appointment to also see the school principal. At this meeting, have the teacher explain what he is doing to provide instruction to the students and ask the principal what she is doing to get the books to the school. Wait and hear the explanations. Many programs do not necessarily use a textbook on a daily basis, but supplement the course with other resources and materials. This may also be the case with your child's classes. The bottom line is that the school is providing your child the high-quality education that all children need and deserve.

School has been in session for several weeks now and my child is still missing many of the necessary textbooks, even though the school board has a policy that every student will have one. I am concerned that he is missing out on important information. What should I do?

Parent-to-Parent Tip:

Get to know your school policy on textbooks. Are textbooks mandatory in all classes or are they used as a supplement and a resource to classroom instruction? If textbooks are mandatory and each child must have one, work with the school principal in trying to expedite fulfillment of the book order as soon as possible. One recommendation you could make is that the principal call other schools in the area and ask to borrow a "class set" of books until the order comes in. You can help out by volunteering to go to these other schools, picking up the books, and being responsible for seeing that they are returned when they are no longer needed.

You are your child's best advocate.

Snapshot #17:

The School Bus Is Failing to Pick Up My Child

My son began to ride the school bus to school this year. During the first month of school, everything went well, but now the school bus has forgotten to pick up my child at least three times this week. Because of this, he has arrived late to school. I am a working parent and cannot continue to take him since this is making me late to work, too. I have tried to call the transportation department to speak to the driver, but have not been able to speak to her. The transportation dispatcher said she would look into the problem, but I have not seen any changes. What should I do?

Tip:

Elementary/Middle/High:
If your child rides a public school district bus, call the school principal or assistant principal and tell the school what is happening. Follow this phone call with a letter to the principal. Inform the school of your concerns and what you have done to try to fix the problem. Ask the principal to give you a call about what he has done to provide solutions to this problem. Usually a phone call from the principal to the transportation department of the school district should clear up the situation immediately.

If, however, your child rides a private bus, you will have to call the owner of the bus company and file an official complaint. If you cannot get this problem fixed, you may have to switch to a different private bus company.

Be a good listener, then determine your course of action.

46

Snapshot #18:
I Must Drop Off My Child Very Early at School

I have just started a new job that requires me to begin work at 7:00 a.m. I have been dropping off my child at school before I go to work. The school principal just called and told me that I can no longer drop him off this early. I'd like to know why I can't. This is the only way I can get my child to school and still be to work on time. What should I do?

Tip:

Elementary:

Your first concern is that you do not want to drop off your child if there is no supervision at the school that early. Call the principal and ask to meet with her. If your schedule does not allow a face-to-face meeting, ask to talk to her about this concern on the phone. Let the principal know of your new work schedule and ask her for other alternatives that the school might have. Many schools have a before- and after-school care program for children of working parents. This program is usually run by the school or another organization for a fee to the parents. If you have a financial hardship, you may qualify for a reduced fee or a complete waiver of the fee. Other alternatives are to ask a relative or a trusted friend to take your child to school or perhaps drop your child at a schoolmate's house so that they can go to school together. You want your child to be supervised by an adult at all times and dropping him off at school early can pose a threat to his safety.

Middle/High:

Dropping off a child at school at 6:45 a.m. when school does not start until 8:30 a.m. is not wise, especially when no school personnel are scheduled to supervise the children. Many middle schools also have before- and after-school care programs. Ask the school for the supervision procedures and the time. Know what time school starts for your child.

> **Students should always be properly supervised.**

Snapshot #19:

My Child's Books Are Too Heavy For Her to Carry

Why aren't there lockers at school? My child's spine is starting to curve. Every day she carries a set of books for each subject, plus her normal school supplies, in her backpack. The backpack has become so heavy that often I can't even carry it. She says that the teachers want the students to bring all books to class in case the lesson that day is from the book. This is ridiculous. My child's posture is suffering. What should I do?

Tip:

Elementary:

Find out the school policy on this. If your daughter is having back problems, get a doctor's note and present it to the school. Then work on reaching a compromise. Ask if two sets of books could be issued to your child—one set to be kept in the classroom, the other set for home. Listen for the reasoning. The school may not be able to afford two sets of books. Ask if there are other solutions, such as the teacher keeping the books in school and only sending home those necessary for homework, posting the homework on the school website, or using other websites for assignments. There are plenty of free sites with practice sheets, and the book publisher itself may have a site for worksheets and follow-up lessons. Many publishers also provide textbooks on CD-ROM.

www.school-talk.com

A study conducted by doctors at Johns Hopkins University in Baltimore, Maryland, found that many students did not carry their backpacks correctly.

Make sure your child:
1. Has well-padded shoulder straps.
2. Uses both straps to carry the backpack.
3. Does not sling the backpack over one shoulder.
4. Only carries necessary items.

> # A good-quality education program is geared to meet all students' needs.

Tip : **Middle/High:**
If your daughter's physician feels she may suffer permanent damage, ask him to write a note to the effect that she cannot carry more than a certain weight every day. This should prompt the school to accommodate her. Also ask if she can be given an extra set of books to keep at home. You may want to ask about lockers, and why they aren't used anymore. However, the principal will likely tell you that because of the recent acts of violence in schools nationwide, lockers have been eliminated, as they have been used to store weapons and drugs. Sit down with the school staff and see if there are any other alternatives. You may suggest books on floppy disks or CDs that students can use in school and at home.

Parent-to-Parent Tip:

Many school districts have a way for parents to purchase additional books for the children to keep at home. If you are interested in this solution, ask the school principal or assistant principal for the specifics, such as the name of each one of your daughter's textbooks, the publishers, and the distributors from whom you can purchase them.

Snapshot #20:

I Am Worried My Child Is Failing

I am concerned about my child's progress and feel like I need more communication on how he is doing. It is not enough to have report cards, progress reports, or a conference once a year. I don't want to upset the teacher by constantly bothering her, but I just don't feel at ease unless I know how my child is doing throughout the school year. What should I do?

Speak with the teacher at the beginning of the year to set up a plan on how to communicate about your child's progress.

Tip :

Elementary:

Set up a meeting with the teacher. Bring with you possible strategies you both can use to alleviate your anxiety while not adding stress to the teacher. Some ideas might include a simple checklist done on a weekly basis or a weekly e-mail. When you do establish your strategy, keep your communications short and to the point. Do not get into a whole history each week, but ask only those questions or address those concerns that are of immediate importance. Your main concern is that your child is making progress and succeeding. Remember, the teacher has at least twenty-five other sets of parents and students with whom she must keep up.

Middle/High:

Explain your situation to the team of teachers. You may want the teachers to give your child a **Weekly Progress Report** as shown on page 51. Make sure your child understands it is his responsibility to hand this report to the teacher and also bring it home to you for signature at the end of the week. If you are more comfortable using a computer, ask that each teacher communicate with you via e-mail and that you will do the same. E-mailing is easier for all concerned, since it can be done whenever it's convenient. If you do not have access to a computer, see if the school has one for parents to use or use the computer at the local library, which should have Internet access.

Weekly Progress Report
Academic Communication Checklist

Directions: Teacher completes the chart on a weekly basis and sends home for parent signature.

Student's Name: _____

Teacher's Name: _____

Week Of: _____

SUBJECT	EXCELLENT	AVERAGE	FAILING	COMMENTS
English				
Math				
Reading				
Science				
Social Studies				
Writing				
Other				

Parent's Signature: _____ **Date:** _____

Parent-to-Parent Tip:

To get your child back on track, talk to the teachers and have them sign a planner or agenda book on a daily basis. In the upper grades, it should be the student's responsibility to bring the planner or agenda book to the teachers for signature. Reading nightly should also be considered as mandatory homework for children at all levels.

Snapshot #21: The School's Pickup and Drop-Off Procedure Is Disorganized

I just lost it. This is the third time one particular parent has gone ahead of me in the carpool lane and almost caused an accident. It's not only rude, it's dangerous. I purposely get there fifteen minutes early to be near the front of the line, yet this woman always arrives late and then cuts in front of me. We've had several parent meetings about this problem. Yet apparently people are still allowed to break the rules and create an unsafe environment for the children. What should I do?

Set an example for your children. Obey all the school rules.

Tip:

Elementary/Middle/High:
Keep your cool in front of your children. Explain to them why rules are important and that there are ways to solve problems calmly and without fighting. Seek out the teacher or administrator in charge. Let him know how concerned you are about this parent's behavior and that you feel her lack of concern for the rules may cause an injury or accident. File a written complaint in the office if you have to, but make sure you don't go unnoticed. Come up with some suggestions on how the carpool lanes could be used more effectively. Some ideas are: staggering pickup times by grade levels; having siblings meet and stand in the carpool area together so the parent doesn't have to stop twice; putting labels in the car with children's and teachers' names; or giving each grade a color-coded card so the students will know where to stand. Set up an exact place for your child to meet you. Ask him not to be late. In many middle and high schools, police officers assist in the traffic patterns for the arrival and dismissal of students. It is the school's responsibility to make sure that all parents follow appropriate procedures. If this is of concern, you may want to talk to the principal or go directly to the police officer and place your complaint. Helpful hints are always welcomed if they can ease the traffic situation.

Snapshot #22:

My Child Is Not Getting Enough Homework

I spoke with my neighbor whose child is in the same grade as mine, but in another school. Her daughter seems to have homework nightly, while my child hardly gets any. When I approached the teacher, she said that she assigns homework every night, as that is the school's policy. I was shocked and told her that I know for a fact my child does nothing at home and she constantly tells me she has no homework. What should I do?

Tip :

Elementary:

Apologize for overreacting at the last meeting. Meet with the teacher and explain your concern again.

Have the teacher go over the curriculum—that is, what is being taught and what your child needs to learn for the school year—and what is expected of the students. If, indeed, homework is assigned every night, then you need to talk about the situation. Ask what your daughter does in class and whether she's copying down the assignments. Tell the teacher you check the planner daily, but it doesn't always have something written for every day of the week. Also ask the teacher about how she runs the class, her policies, and her routines. After your initial discussion, you may want to call in your child so you can review what was decided and make sure your child understands. Be sure your child knows that you are passionate about getting homework done and that you feel that it is of the utmost importance. Again, a system may need to be developed so your child gets on the right homework track. Ask the teacher to team with you to check homework assignments daily. You may want to use the **Homework Checklist for School Success** and the **Homework Scheduler** on pages 54–55.

Middle/High:

Meet with the teachers in the team, if possible. Make sure you understand each one's homework policy and that your child knows them as well. Have your child present at the meeting. Be prepared to listen and to come away from the meeting with a workable solution.

Explain to your daughter how concerned you are and that you will be checking to make sure that her homework is completed on its due date and handed in on time.

If no homework is assigned on a given night, let your daughter know you expect her to read and review her class notes so she is well prepared for quizzes and other assignments.

> *Wait for explanations. Never overreact or lose your temper, especially in front of your children. Remember, you are a role model for your child.*

Homework Checklist for School Success

☐ **My child has a homework area that is a quiet place to do homework, one without distractions from the television, other family members, or video games.**

☐ **My child has a desk/table with good lighting.**

☐ **My child has all of the supplies needed—pens, pencils, crayons, scissors, glue—in his homework area so that time is not wasted looking for these supplies.**

☐ **My child does homework at the same time every day.**

☐ **My child has a homework schedule/calendar and follows it daily.**

☐ **My child has a snack before doing homework so being hungry cannot be used as an excuse to avoid doing the homework.**

☐ **My child uses a timer.**

☐ **Other** _____

_____

Parent's Signature: **Date:**

Homework should not be an all-night project. If it is, schedule a conference with the teacher and ask the following questions:

1. How much time should my child spend doing homework?
2. Does unfinished class work become homework?
3. Is there homework assigned every night in every subject?
4. How can I work with my child at home?

You want to make sure that your child is understanding what is being taught in class. Homework reinforces class lessons. Work with the teacher as a team.

More Tips . . .
1. Remember, homework is the child's work.
2. A parent's role is that of advisor and checker.
3. Write a note or phone the teacher if your child doesn't seem to understand a concept.
4. Praise your child's effort and good work.
5. If your child says his homework was done in class, check it.
6. If he says there is no homework and it goes on for several days, ask the teacher. Don't assume that the child is always telling the truth.

Homework Scheduler

On the calendar below put the time that your child does homework daily. A section has also been provided for special projects and reports so that you can track them ahead of time.

Month: **Year:**

Sunday	Monday	Tuesday	Wednesday	Thursday	Friday	Saturday

Special Projects/Reports	Due Date
1.	
2.	
3.	
4.	
5.	
6.	
7.	
8.	
9.	
10.	
11.	
12.	
13.	
14.	
15.	
16.	
17.	
18.	
19.	
20	
21.	
22.	
23.	
24.	

Snapshot #23:
The Teacher Can't Write Correctly

My child has been bringing home term papers, book reports, and his daily writing assignments with comments from the teacher, and, frankly, I'm appalled. The teacher has more spelling and grammatical errors in her comments than my child does in his school papers, and many of the "errors" the teacher circled were actually correct. How can she be teaching my child how to write when she can't even write herself? This is one area in which I would like to see my child improve, as I think his writing skills are weak. What should I do?

Tip:

Elementary/Middle/High:
In this case, you may want to go directly to the principal. Request a conference and bring the papers that show the incorrect comments. Explain why you feel this is not acceptable, and ask that the problem be resolved. Have a deadline in mind and follow up with the principal again if this situation does not get better. Offer a solution that will satisfy you and help your child. Stress that your child needs to receive instruction that will improve his writing ability, not hinder it. Make the focus of your conversation be that your child needs a good role model. This is important to your child's future; be his advocate.

Save all work sent home and bring the samples to conferences.

56

Snapshot #24:

My Child Is Fifteen Minutes Late to Class Daily

Every day the school attendance monitor calls to report that my child is missing from fourth period, only to call later to let me know that he showed up fifteen to twenty minutes late. I'm concerned about this chronic tardiness. What should I do?

Parent-to-Parent Tip:

Fifteen to twenty minutes is a very long time for a child to be unsupervised at school. Get to the root of the problem immediately and ask your child, "What is really going on?" If this is happening every day, a number of issues may come to the surface. Be ready for some serious discussions with your child.

Tip :

Elementary:

Speak to your child and let him know you will no longer tolerate this behavior. Make it clear he will have to make up the work he missed and that the teacher may not give him a passing grade if this continues. Tell him attendance is essential in all classes. You will not accept any excuses for tardiness. Next, speak to the teacher. Let her know that your child may need to be monitored when he changes for his fourth-period class. Assure her that you have told your son that he will suffer consequences if he continues to come late to class.

Middle/High:

Make it clear to your child that school comes first, and that arriving late for class is not acceptable. Point out that he will fail the course due to time missed in class and his incomplete assignments. Sit him down and do the math: fifteen minutes each day, five days a week equals seventy-five minutes lost each week; seventy-five minutes each week equals 300 minutes or five hours per month. Maybe if he sees that he is missing the equivalent of one whole day of instruction each month, he will realize why his grade is not as high as it should be. Not only is he penalizing himself by jeopardizing his grades, the school may want to give him detention to make up the time missed as well as not give him a passing grade. Let him know you plan to give him a consequence at home, too. For every minute of class time missed, you can double that and deduct it from his allotted time on the phone. However, don't forget to reward him if his behavior improves. If he stops being tardy, those minutes can be added back to the phone time.

> *School is important. Insist on punctuality or give consequences at home.*

Snapshot #25:
My Child's Homework Takes Up Too Much Time

I am spending too much time with my child on homework. I thought homework was simply a review and should be completed in a reasonable amount of time. Many times, it just appears to be busywork. I'm overstressed and my child never has any downtime just to relax. What should I do?

Meeting With the Teacher on Homework

You have scheduled a meeting to discuss your child's homework concerns. Go prepared. Bring suggestions with you. Below are several ideas you can bring to the meeting:

1. Bring the **Homework Scheduler** to the meeting. Make sure the calendar is filled in with the time your child does homework daily.

2. Ask what the recommended time limit is for each subject per night.

3. Ask the teacher if she knows of a homework hotline, any websites, and educational software that maybe useful. The bottom line is to work as a team!

Tip :

Elementary:
Set up an appointment with the teacher as soon as possible. Don't let it go on too long; this is a serious problem the teacher needs to address immediately to help you and your child. The teacher should show you her homework policy and a typical day's work. Ask if your child is taking home work she didn't finish in class; whether she is grasping all the concepts taught; if the homework focuses on new skills or reviews skills taught in class. Continue to ask your child and yourself the following questions: Does my child comprehend the work? Is she staying focused in class? Is she as well prepared as she could be for school? Once these questions are answered, both of you and the teacher can work on solutions. Reporting to each other on whether the solutions are working will keep stress down for everyone. If the strategies are not working, try new ones. You may want to use **Homework Checklist for School Success** on page 54 and the **Homework Scheduler** on page 55 to keep your child on track.

Middle/High:
First discuss with your child why she thinks the homework is taking up so much of her free time at home. Make sure she gets in the habit of copying down assignments, projects, and tests for each class in a planner or agenda. Set up an appointment with all her teachers so a solution can be worked out. Make sure she participates in discussing and planning the solutions.

Snapshot #26:

The School Newspaper Has Grammatical Errors

The school sent home its very first newspaper completed by the newly formed journalism club. I read it as soon as it arrived home, because my child is one of the reporters. However, I was shocked to see so many spelling and grammatical errors and was surprised that the principal allowed this to be sent home without being corrected. What should I do?

Always check your written communications for errors.

Tip :

Elementary:

Call the teacher responsible for the journalism club and ask for an appointment to discuss the newspaper. You may want to give him the **Request for Conference Letter** on page 60. Bring the newspaper with you and circle the errors you discovered.

Make it clear you are using it as a reference point for discussion. From there ask him how you may be of assistance so the school newspaper can reflect the children's talent and best work. Perhaps you could offer to edit the next edition, or you may offer to come in and show the children how to check their work. You may suggest a field trip to a local paper to let the children see all the steps involved in turning out a real newspaper, so the children can gain pride in their own work.

Middle/High:

Bring the newspaper in and show it to the teacher in charge of the journalism club. Tell him you are upset at the many mistakes, and explain to him that you put your child in the club for experience and camaraderie, but also to learn how to use the computer, spell correctly, and write well. Explain your concerns that this first edition did not meet your expectations and offer your help to the teacher. Don't forget to listen to his side of the story, which may offer more insight. There may have been a problem with the computer program, the children's eagerness could have overshadowed the importance for quality work, or perhaps they had to rush to meet the deadline. Whatever the scenario, you should try offering suggestions or even your assistance to the teacher so the quality of the next newspaper is high, reflecting everyone's hard work and pride in their product. You may want to suggest that if the club turns out high-quality work, you could find a contest in which to enter the newspaper. A search on the Internet will probably yield that information. Giving the children that kind of incentive usually draws the best out of them.

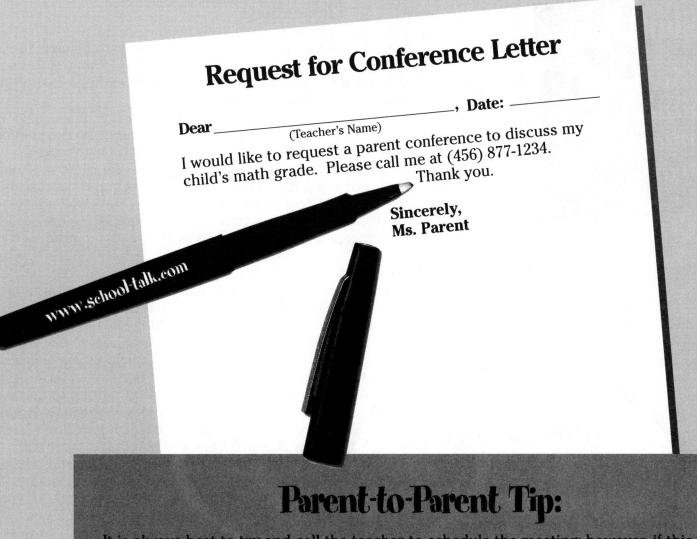

Request for Conference Letter

Dear _____, **Date:** _____
(Teacher's Name)

I would like to request a parent conference to discuss my child's math grade. Please call me at (456) 877-1234.
Thank you.

Sincerely,
Ms. Parent

Parent-to-Parent Tip:

It is always best to try and call the teacher to schedule the meeting; however, if this is not possible, send a letter with your child or fax the letter to school. If you have not heard from the teacher within 48 hours, call the school.

Snapshot #27:
The School Cafeteria Never Has Any Variety

The students never get a choice of menu. This is the second time in the same week that the school cafeteria has given the children hot dogs. My child does not like hot dogs; she didn't eat a full lunch on either day and came home hungry. I feel the school should provide a more nutritious lunch and offer the child a choice. What should I do?

Tip:

Elementary:
Many schools offer the students a choice of either a hot lunch or a sandwich. Call or go and speak to the cafeteria manager or school administration about your concern. They can clarify what the choices are and assist you with the school lunch procedures. Ask the staff whether they can provide you with the upcoming week's menu. Many schools post this on their website. If your child does not like the food choice on a particular day, pack a lunch or at least a snack to accompany the school lunch program.

Middle/High:
Many middle and high schools offer food choices other than a hot lunch and a sandwich. Some offer pizza and snacks on a daily basis. Talk to your child about good nutrition, and then give her the responsibility for making her food choices. Monitor what she eats. If she has a hard time eating right with all the food choices available, have her pack a lunch.

P.S.: Practice *What to Say* When They Say...

> **"Doing all of this homework is a waste of time, and I just don't get it."**

> **"I hate school. The teacher is always picking on me. I don't like the other kids. I couldn't care less about the schoolwork. Besides, I stink at it."**

"This is an important issue. Are you clear on the information taught in the school lessons? Is the teacher assisting you when things are not clear in class? Do you understand the assignment? Are you letting the teacher know that you are having difficulty? Let's find a time every night where we can go over the daily work together and see where the problems are for you. I am here to help. I want to know exactly what is going on. Perhaps you and I and maybe the teacher can work together so the school work becomes less stressful."

OR

"Homework is an important part of your learning. It's a useful tool in helping you review what you were taught in the classroom each day."

"Are you having trouble understanding the information the teacher gives you in his lessons? Does the teacher help you when things are not clear in class? Do you let him know when you are having a difficult time? Do you understand what he wants when he gives out the homework assignment?"

"Let's find a time every night when we can go over the daily work together and see where the problems are for you. I am here to help, but to do that, I need to know exactly what is going on. Perhaps you and I can meet with the teacher to solve this problem. I'm sure if we work together, the schoolwork will become less difficult and stressful."

"I know that the teacher is on you a great deal. That's because she cares about you and wants you to achieve success, and so do I."

"What's really the problem here? Do you simply not understand the work? Is there some student who is bothering you? Are you having some other problem I don't know about? Let's sit down and talk about it. I'm here to help you. I want to hear what you have to say so we can solve this problem together. Once we know exactly what the difficulties are, your teacher and I can try to find a solution so that you can enjoy and do well at school."

Notes:

SECTION THREE: WINTER
Stay on Target – Keep the Lines of Communication Open

"The dream begins with a teacher who believes in you, who tugs and pushes and leads you into the next plateau, sometimes poking you with a sharp stick called truth."
Dan Rather

Snapshot #28: My Child Does Not Enjoy Reading

My son never picks up a book, and he finishes any homework he might have as quickly as possible. He gets home before I do, and by the time I open the door, he says he's done with his homework and wants to go play or call his friends. After working all day, I'm busy at night preparing dinner and doing other household chores, so I don't have time to look over his homework. I am worried that he won't keep up and do well in school with the attitude he has. What should I do?

Parent-to-Parent Tip:

Encourage reading at home. Get a library card for each family member. Make plans to visit the library or your local bookstore as part of your weekend family time. Make it a positive family activity and get a treat afterwards. Act as a role model for your child by checking out a book for yourself, then letting your child see you read it. Help your child pick out books that interest him at his reading level. Check with the teacher for a suggested list of book titles and authors. Know the hours of your local library. Get a calendar of special events that are going on and make it a point to visit during those times.

Tip:

Elementary:
No matter how rough your day was and no matter how tired you are, set aside a time, at least fifteen minutes, to talk with your child. A good time to do this is while you are preparing dinner. Ask your child to show you the homework he did and to share his day with you. This is important, so that you can keep up with what he is learning and monitor his grades. After dinner, turn the television off and either read together or separately. If you show him that you read for enjoyment and that television is not as important as a book, he might just follow your example. Phone calls and housework can wait a few minutes. **The quality—not the quantity—of time spent together is what's important.**

Be a role model for your child.

Tip: **Middle/High:**
Even though your child is in the upper grades, it is still important for you, the parent, to check that he is completing his work. Do not wait until that school report card comes home. Review his planner and his work. Ask questions about school. Keep on top of his school requirements and whether he is fulfilling them as he should. Make a point of turning off the television in your home. Stress to your son through example that reading for pleasure or for schoolwork is more important. You might suggest to your child that he can start with reading a comic book as long as he is reading. Show that reading has a high priority for you. Read when your child does. Perhaps you could set aside a time every day for reading as part of the family's schedule.

Simple Strategies for Creating Strong Readers

• **Invite your child to read with you every day.**

• **Read your child's favorite book over and over.**

• **Stop and ask about the pictures and about what is happening in the story.**

Source: Reading Tips for Parents, U.S. Department of Education.

For more information call:
1-800-USA-LEARN

Snapshot #29:
My Child's Behavior Has Changed Since He Left Elementary School

My son was a straight-A student in elementary school. When he started middle school/junior high, he completely changed. When he comes home from school each day, he goes straight to his room, saying nothing to me or his brother. He suddenly wants to wear only black and doesn't care about his appearance. Today the school called to say he is failing three classes and was caught skipping school. What should I do?

Tip :

Elementary/Middle/High:

Many children have a hard time adjusting as they move from elementary to middle school and from middle to high, especially if the school is much larger and there are new friends to deal with. Help your child with the transition by keeping the lines of communication open. You may also want to talk to the school counselor about how he can help all of the children have an easy transition into middle school and ask for some tips you can use with your child specifically.

Do not confront your child; be a good listener. Let your child know you are concerned about his behavior and that you are to there help. Call the school and meet with the counselor. Voice your concerns. Ask the counselor if the school has a program to deal with the behaviors that your child is exhibiting. Many children will be angry and not want to talk to you or to have the parent help in any way. If this is the case, call a trained professional who deals with pre-teen and teen issues and behaviors. The school should be able to direct you to a program. Many programs work on a sliding-fee scale if you do not have insurance.

> *Be available to talk at any time. STOP what you are doing and give your child your full attention. Your child comes first.*

Parent-to-Parent Tip:

Your child is having a difficult time dealing with some issues, and the sooner you take action, the better it will be for everyone. Make an appointment to see the school counselor immediately and ask about getting your child into a counseling program. Because middle school is so different from elementary, some children can become stressed and depressed at the change. Do not dismiss this as "simply a phase." Some children will begin to go into a deeper depression if the behavior is not dealt with appropriately. Remember, if you get your child outside professional help, make sure you are consistent with the appointments and your child is comfortable with the counselor. You may also want to join a parent support group. Sometimes the best advice and references are from other parents who have been there and have helped turn around their children's behavior.

Snapshot #30:
My Child Gets Sick Every Day at the Same Time

The school calls almost every day by third or fourth period to say that my child is complaining of a headache and suggesting I should come and pick him up. I work and I can't take time off to come and get him. His eyes have been checked and are fine, and the medical doctor says there is nothing wrong with him. What should I do?

Always seek out the source of the problem.

Tip:

Elementary:
Try to find out the real cause of this problem. Talk to your child. Ask him questions about his day at school. Find out what goes on before, during, and after the time that he feels ill. Is someone picking on him? Ask whether there might be something bothering him at school. If the headaches occur at the same time every day, maybe he doesn't like the subject taught during that period, such as math or physical education. You may want to set up a conference with the teacher to get her insight or ask the school counselor to assist you with this problem. If you can't find any good reason for the headaches, inform your child and the school that he is to stay in class. Education is your child's top priority, and unless he has something physically wrong with him that can be recognized by the teacher or diagnosed by a doctor, there is no reason for him to come home.

Middle/High:
Try calling the school for a conference with school personnel. Maybe your child is avoiding a particular class period because of the teacher, a classmate, or the subject matter. If this is the case, seek the help of the school administration and the counselor. Try to find solutions to the problem at hand. A last resort may be to ask for your child to be moved to a different teacher and class altogether if the problem cannot be solved. If no reason is readily apparent and it appears that your child just wants to go home or skip school, then you need to stress the importance of going to class, pulling good grades, and creating an opportunity for a bright future. Taking care of the situation as soon as possible will emphasize that going to school is your child's main job and you want him to succeed at that job. Both good grades and attendance are factors in receiving a passing grade and making it to graduation, which should be your child's long-term goal. If he does not attend his classes, then make it clear you will impose consequences.

Snapshot #31:
My Child's Classmate Threatened to Bring a Gun to School

I'm extremely worried. My son came home and told me that one of his classmates was really upset with the teacher and threatened to bring a gun to school. What should I do?

Tip:

Elementary/Middle/High:
Many times students will make outrageous statements to fellow classmates. However, threatening to bring a weapon to school can never be ignored. Make it clear to your child that when he hears such a threat, he should immediately tell the closest adult to him. Most school districts have zero tolerance for bringing weapons to school. Emphasize to your child that this is not being a tattletale, but a responsible student and good citizen. If you are the first adult your child tells, you have the responsibility to notify the principal immediately. While more and more schools are using metal detectors, identification systems, and even drug-sniffing dogs, the best system is still good communication between the students and the adults. Weapons seldom come into a school facility without some significant red flags going up through a student's words or actions. All students must feel a responsibility to their peers to maintain a safe learning environment.

Speak-Up!

Speak-Up is a national campaign that encourages students to anonymously report gun threats in their school.

Call 1-866-SPEAK-UP

**For more information on Speak-Up
Visit: www.pax.com**

Snapshot #32:
I Never Know What Is Happening at the School

I met a neighbor at the supermarket whose child is in my daughter's class. She asked why I hadn't attended the parent breakfast. She went on to say how great it was and that my child received a certificate for a poem she wrote. I knew nothing about it and was terribly upset at having missed the event. What should I do?

Tip:

Elementary:
Teachers typically let parents know well ahead of time about such events. Check your child's backpack regularly for flyers and reminder notes. Read all notices that come home; you can also look at the school's website and any e-mails that you have received. Listen to your child when she tells you about upcoming events, and ask her each day what's going on in school. As soon as you know about an event, mark your calendar and make every effort to attend. This sends the message to your child that her education comes first. School activities should be just as important and well attended as sports events and weekly practices. If the school sends out a weekly or monthly calendar with activities, you may want to post this in an area in your home that is easy to see. A good place is on the refrigerator.

Middle/High:
If you carpool, check the school marquee, and look for notices about special award days and evening events on the school's website. It is important to be just as involved in your child's education when she's in the upper grades as it was while she attended elementary school. No matter what their age, children enjoy sharing their accomplishments with family members. Make sure you place the same importance on school events as you do on sports events, so that your child knows that education is a priority for her.

> **Make time for school events. Show your child where your priorities lie.**

Parent-to-Parent Tip:
Find out why your child didn't tell you about the event. The reason may surprise you!

71

Snapshot #33:

My Child Wrote on a Wall After Being Influenced by His Peers

My child came home and told me he got into trouble today at school and received a consequence for his actions. He had followed another student into the bathroom who brought out a permanent marker and wrote inappropriate words on the wall. This boy then challenged my son to write some words too "if he wasn't too scared." A teacher came in just as my son was writing on the wall. He issued my son a detention and gave him a rag to wash the graffiti off the wall. The writing did not come off. My son saw nothing wrong with what he did, since it was not his idea and there were other writings on the wall. Why was he singled out? What should I do?

Tip:

Elementary:

Speak to your child about the choice he made. Explain that writing on the wall is a serious offense, because he caused damage to the school property. Back up the school in the discipline action that was given. Next, have a discussion with him about yielding to peer pressure. Point out that although this time no one was harmed, the next time he follows a bad idea something more serious could occur. Emphasize that it takes more courage to walk away from something he knows is wrong than to just follow along with what everyone else is doing. Tell him you expect him to be strong enough to say "NO" to a dare or to participating in an act he knows is wrong. Role-play or practice the scene. This will make your child more confident in facing this type of situation and making the right choice.

Behavior Contract

Date: _____

I, _____ , promise to

_____

_____

_____

By_____

Date to see changes

Signed: Parent:_____

Teacher:_____

Student:_____

Teach your child to make positive decisions.

Tip :

Middle/High:

Make an appointment to have a meeting with your child and the necessary school personnel. In the meeting, show your support for the school's rules and discipline. If your child was caught in a wrongful act, then he deserves to suffer appropriate consequences at school. Next, decide what consequences will be delivered at home. Maybe taking his allowance away or having him do some work at school to help pay for the paint to cover up the words would be appropriate. The goal is to have your child become a responsible citizen.

Parent-to-Parent Tip:

The more important issue for your child is that of making appropriate decisions for himself and not blindly following others who make a wrong decision. Telling your child to walk away from a wrongful act, to stand firm and not be swayed by peer pressure, is the best advice you can give. Remind your child to think ahead, to consider what will happen if he gets caught, and to think about how he will be penalized for his actions in a way that may be not only painful to him, but may negatively affect his future. Emphasize that even though no one was harmed in this incident, next time that may not be the case. Keep the lines of communication open with your child. Talk to him every night and encourage him to come to you with problems. Peer pressure is very prevalent in the upper grades and your child needs you to establish and clarify values and offer guidance more than ever if he is to succeed.

Snapshot #34:

The Teacher Is Picking on My Child

Once again, the first words from my child's mouth when she gets home from school are that the teacher picked on her. She complained that the teacher singled her out when she was with a group of children who were talking. Last week, she got in trouble for gum-chewing, even though she told me all her friends were chewing gum after lunch. I'd like to know why the teacher told only my child to stop and throw it out. The other day my daughter said the teacher yelled at her to stay in line. I am tired of my child being picked on when she is not the only one who seems to be disobeying the rules. What should I do?

Always seek out the source of the problem and try to come to a resolution.

Tip :

Elementary:
The first step might be to have your daughter approach the teacher in a friendly but concerned manner to explain how she feels. Explain to your daughter that having a discussion is the proper way to solve a situation that bothers her. Role-play the discussion with her so she can feel comfortable addressing the teacher. If that doesn't work out, set up an appointment with the teacher. You may want to use the **Request for Conference Letter** on page 60. At that meeting, discuss how your child feels she is being picked on unfairly and that you'd like to hear the teacher's observations. You might learn a lot more about some of the behaviors your child has described. The same situation, when described from the teacher's point of view, might be quite different from that of your child. Whatever the case, a solution needs to be determined. Once you and the teacher have reached an agreement, call your daughter in to the discussion and share the outcome with her. Remember that all three of you need to be open and honest so you can move on and make the rest of the year successful and happy.

Changing That Behavior Worksheet

Parent's Name: _____
Child's Name: _____

Date of Conference: _____
Problem: _____
_____
_____
_____
_____
_____
_____

How My Child Tried to Solve the Problem in School:
Date: _____
_____
Date: _____
_____
Date: _____
_____

How My Child and I Tried to Resolve the Problem at Home:
Date: _____
_____
Date: _____
_____
Date: _____
_____

Possible New Suggestions: _____
_____
_____
_____
_____
_____

www.schooltalk.com

Tip : **Middle/High:**
Role-play with your child how she is to talk with the teacher about this problem in a calm and mature manner. Have her ask for an appointment before or after school to discuss the problem. Suggest that she tell the teacher she feels she's being picked on, and then have her ask what they both can do to remedy this situation. Make sure your daughter is willing to be open to what the teacher has to say. The teacher may view this scenario entirely differently than your daughter does. In any case, let your daughter know that she and the teacher must come up with a workable solution so that both are agreeable on the outcome. If this doesn't work, praise your daughter for trying. Then you may need to go up to see the teacher and work out a solution between the two of you. After the meeting, if a solution is achieved, share it with your daughter. If this doesn't work and your daughter still complains, write the problem down and what you have done to try and resolve it. Use the **Changing That Behavior** worksheet at the right to help you.

Snapshot #35:

A Disruptive Classmate Is Hitting My Child

I went marching into the principal's office, really mad. It was obvious to me that all the complaints I had made to the teacher about Johnny hitting my daughter and other girls in class were being ignored. I know the teacher had moved Johnny to a seat near her desk, but the hitting still goes on. I feel the teacher is ineffective and this child is completely out of control. I think he should be removed, as he is disruptive to the class and frightening to my daughter and other students. What should I do?

Tip :

Elementary/Middle/High:

Storming into the principal's office may hurt rather than help your cause. No matter how angry you are, call first for an appointment. Once inside the principal's office, state your concerns, describe what you have seen, and explain what, in your opinion, has not been done. Explain that you have already seen the teacher and that nothing appears to have changed. You want an administrator's input and commitment to clearing up the situation. Also, speak with your child about how to handle these situations. Role-play a scenario where your child acts as the bully and you take her role. This might let your child see how one can best deal with problems without getting into any serious trouble. Emphasize the fact that fighting back does not work, but neither does she have to put up with being terrorized.

Remember, most schools have a zero tolerance policy for any hitting, bullying, or misbehaving. Due to restrictions regarding privacy, the principal may not tell you specifically what has been done, but, hopefully, she can assure you that some corrective action is being taken and that the teacher and other staff are working on the situation.

Parent-to-Parent Tip:

It is always a good idea to call the school principal and set up an appointment to speak about your concerns. However, situations that are extremely important to the safety of the children warrant immediate attention. In cases such as these, you need to go to the school immediately and communicate the problem.

> *Be patient; there may be more to the picture than you are seeing.*

Snapshot #36:

My Child Is Being Suspended for Fighting, While the Child Who Started the Fight Is Not

I just got a phone call from the principal telling me that my child is being suspended from school for slapping another child in his class. I know that this child has been picking on my son, and he probably provoked my son into retaliation. I am a single working mother. I don't have anyone to supervise my son and I cannot take time off of work. Worse yet, the child who verbally attacked my son and started the fight did not get suspended. What should I do?

Tip:

Elementary:

Request a meeting with the principal and the school counselor. Have your child present and ask him to tell them why he slapped the other child. Make it clear that hitting under any circumstance is not permissible and that you will impose your own consequences on him. Does your child have trouble managing his anger? Has he told anyone at the school that this child has been picking on him? Work with the administration and the counselor and come up with a behavioral or anger management plan. Also ask whether the counselor can conduct a mediation to resolve the conflict between the two children. Ask the counselor and the school principal if the school has an indoor suspension program, and if your child could spend the same amount of time in that type of suspension.

Middle/High:

Talk to your child; listen to what he has to say without interrupting. Ask him why he went to the extreme of slapping another student. Meet with the child's teacher and counselor; you can also request to have an administrator present. Have the counselor meet with your child and the other student and do peer mediation to resolve the conflict. First and foremost, your child must understand that hitting will not be tolerated under any circumstances. In some school districts, such action results in the student being expelled from school or a police report filed. Your child should not be taunted by other students and there should be a way for your child to report any harassment. The older your child gets, the more important it is that he learns how to manage his anger. Ask the school for help. Perhaps they have anger management programs or can refer you to outside agencies that will work with your child. Ask whether the school will allow your child to make up the time in an indoor suspension program at the school. By all means, make sure that he does not miss any classwork due to his punishment.

Parent-to-Parent Tip:

As a parent, you must realize that not all children fit into that "perfect child" model. It is your role, along with the school's, to assist our youth to become solid citizens who can successfully participate in society.

77

Snapshot #37:
My Daughter Is Being Sexually Harassed by Another Student

My daughter and her friends are scared to eat lunch in the school cafeteria. There is an older boy who is constantly coming up to them and hugging and kissing them. My daughter has told him to stop, but he has not. She is scared to tell on him for fear that he may retaliate in some way. What should I do?

Tip :

Elementary:
Call the school immediately and meet with the principal. Let the principal know that you also want to speak to the person who is in charge of monitoring your daughter's class in the lunchroom. This may be a security guard, paraprofessional, assistant principal, counselor, or teacher. You and your child need to tell this person what is going on and ask him to keep an eye out for the situation. Instruct your daughter to immediately tell the adult if the situation continues. Role-play with her what she will say and do. Be persistent in your position that you will not tolerate this behavior and you will back her up.

Middle/High:
Immediately ask for a conference with the principal. Work with the school counselor to teach your daughter verbal coping skills so she can ward off anyone who harasses her or gives her unwanted attention. She should also learn how to recognize any threatening situation. Stand your ground that you will not tolerate this situation. Know your rights as a parent within your school and school district.

Parent-to-Parent Tip:

Many schools and school districts have adopted a zero tolerance policy for harassment and have very strict consequences for this type of behavior. Check with your local school and school district and see what your rights are. You must also tell your daughter that she must never allow anyone to harass and intimidate her this way. Call the school counselor, teacher, and school principal and request a meeting immediately. Go to the school the very next day. Do not let this go by. Your daughter needs to learn coping skills to tell this young man to stop, and this young man needs to understand he cannot harass other students. A good idea is to role-play and to strategize with your child on how best to deal with this young man. Practice together until your daughter feels confident enough to stand up for her rights. If the situation is not resolved at the school, you may want to consider taking the matter to the superintendent or school board.

Snapshot #38:

My Child Is Always Getting into Trouble; I Feel the Staff at School Is Picking on Him

Tip : **Elementary/ Middle/High:**
Call the office for a conference with the teacher immediately. Do not wait! Take time off now to address the problem. Show your child that school is a top priority for you, so he will make it a top priority for himself. Work with the teacher and explain the situation at work. With your child present, meet with the teacher and/or an administrator and ask her to help you come up with a plan that will assist your child in changing his behavior. Other staff members may need to be called in to assist in a possible solution. Use the **Behavior Contract** on page 72. Come up with a behavior plan put together by both you and the teacher. You may want to use the **Changing That Behavior** worksheet on page 75 as a guide.

If all of these things are done and the behavior persists, you should request that your child be tested for a learning disability. Ask the principal for information and guidelines on how you can have your child tested to qualify for special assistance or special education.

I am sick and tired of getting phone calls at work from the school staff telling me my child is having a bad day. They call me to say he doesn't complete his work, bothers others, can't stay in his seat, and can't focus. Why can't the staff just handle whatever the problem is? I can't be constantly called at work. My boss is about to let me go. What should I do?

Make it a point to partner with the teacher right from the start.

Parent-to-Parent Tip:

Don't let your child know that you are angry with the school for calling you at work. If phone calls at work are a problem, you may want to give the teacher your cell phone number or the best time for her to call you, for example, during your break time, lunch hour, or after work. Make sure that as far as your child is concerned, you and the school are working together as a team. You are both concerned about his or her inappropriate behavior.

Snapshot #39:
My Child Told Me There Are Drugs in His School

My son came home and told me that the children on the bus were talking about drugs and that certain children said they were selling them in the downstairs bathrooms at school. I was shocked to hear about this information, especially since in the last school newsletter, the principal stated that the school was drug-free. What should I do?

Tip:

Elementary: Tell your son you are proud of him for telling you about the drugs, and that what he did is what we call a "good report." Tell him you want to keep him and his friends well protected and that you will go to the school the first thing in the morning to report the problem. Emphasize that you will make sure that the school keeps his information anonymous.

At school, speak to school staff members and ask that you get a report back from them later in the day on how they handled this problem. Make it clear your position on drugs is zero tolerance. Emphasize that you want your child to remain anonymous for providing the information. Also, strongly recommend that a program on drugs be put into the curriculum. You may suggest that you or they call the local police department to see if an officer can come out and speak about the dangers of drugs and the many terrible consequences of taking or selling them.

Project D.A.R.E.
Drug Abuse Resistance Education

D.A.R.E. provides children with information and skills they need to live drug-free and violence-free lives.

http://www.dare.com

Certain information warrants immediate attention.

Tip :

Middle/High:
Many schools already have a method for children to report delicate situations, while at the same time remaining anonymous. Go to the school the very next day and ask if they have this procedure in place. Explain to your child that you are proud that he knew to come to you with this information, and that you know it is extremely difficult for him to tell on his classmates. He may not want to give names, because he may fear retaliation. Let the school staff tell you how to proceed so that your child remains anonymous. Also, have the administrator report to you later in the day on how the school followed up with this information and what they intend to do about it to prevent any future incidents. Make the point that even if this is just a case of children bragging about taking drugs when they actually don't, you think there should be programs in the school about drugs, their harmful effects, and their disastrous consequences. Ask that the school look into field trips to drug rehabilitation centers and drug enforcement units, or bringing in experts to speak to the students, so the children can see up close the realistic side effects of using drugs.

www.school-talk.com

Snapshot #40:

My Child Got Three F's on His Report Card

I received the latest interim report four weeks ago, which showed my son's grades had slipped. At no time did I ever think he would get three F's on his report card. I came to the realization he may not go on to the next grade if this pattern continues. He started off the year on a positive note: completing assignments, doing classwork, completing homework, and handing in all reports. It seems that he has begun to fall behind the rest of the class. My child doesn't seem to care until I step in, yelling, threatening, and punishing him. What should I do?

Parent-to-Parent Tip:

Stay enthusiastic about school all year long. Encourage and praise your child's efforts, as well as his grades. Yelling and screaming at your child will not do you or your child any good. Instead, sit and listen to what your child says about his failing grades. Set a plan to monitor your child and work with the teacher. Let your child know that you care about his grades and that you expect his best at all times. Offer assistance anytime you become aware of a change in grades and attitude.

Tip :

Elementary:
Ask for a conference with the teaching staff. Explain your child's past history of starting the school year doing his very best and then slowly falling off the targeted goals for success, even though you know he can accomplish the goals with little effort. Ask for advice on how to keep him motivated to do well in school. Teaming up with the teacher the minute you notice a change in the grades will help both of you to stay on top of the situation. Don't wait until a report card comes out. React immediately. After your strategies are worked out, bring the child into the meeting. By doing this, you will let him know you and the teacher are united in your decision and that you both will be monitoring him closely. You may want to use the **Weekly Progress Report Checklist** on page 51 to keep your child on track.

Middle/High:
Follow the information above, but add to your conversation with your child that he must take on the responsibility of monitoring and completing his schoolwork and homework, if he plans to graduate from high school on time and move on to higher education. If leaving it in your child's hands doesn't work, you, as the adult, may need to take an active stand and check repeatedly with his teachers to see if the pattern of lower grades has changed or not.

Snapshot #41:

I Don't Understand the Results from My Child's Standardized Test

Tip :

Elementary/Middle/High:
Call the teacher or school counselor and request a meeting for her to go over the standardized test scores and explain the results to you. Have her come up with a "snapshot" of how your child is doing academically. An example is to look at report card grades, the standardized test scores, homework, classwork, and reading level as a whole. Make a chart and refer to it year after year. If your child is on target, let him know how proud you are of his accomplishments. If your child is behind academically, set up a plan of action with the school for your child to succeed.

M y child just came home and handed me a sheet with the results of the school's standardized test. To tell you the truth, I have no idea how to read this report or how to tell whether my child achieved a passing score. I am concerned since I know how important this is. I want to call the school, but at the same time, I don't want to sound dumb. What should I do?

Understand the requirements for the standardized test. Some states require a child to pass in order to be promoted to the next grade level or graduate from high school.

Continue to monitor school work year-round, no matter what grade your child is in. Ask questions about school and keep in contact with the teachers to discourage a pattern of disinterest.

Tests!
So many tests, so much data.
What is a parent to do?

The best thing to do is visit this website:
www.ed.gov/parent

Snapshot #42:
The Teacher Gives Too Many Projects

E very time I turn around, my child has another project due. We just finished a book report and now he has a science fair project due. Next week he has a presentation to give. This is just too much work and I can't do it anymore. I work and don't have time to do the art portion and the typing. Why are all these extra assignments necessary when he also gets homework every night? What should I do?

www.school-talk.com

Establish routines at home to reduce stress.

Tip :

Elementary:
Don't stop the teacher in the hallway to talk about this. Make an appointment. Explain how you are stressed with all the additional projects and time they require. Wait and hear the justification the teacher gives. You may or may not agree, but at least your opinion will be heard. The teacher may also have a simple reason for assigning the various projects—that some children excel in the oral presentation portion of an assignment rather than the written. Since students have many different learning styles, it is her job to support them all. She may explain that these kinds of projects are assigned well in advance, allowing for some planning.

Your child still needs to accomplish all the work. Time management is the key. Setting up a calendar on the refrigerator and circling the date the science fair project or presentation is due may help your child work on the project a little each night, so that it's not all left to the last minute. Also set aside time on the weekend for you to do any shopping for the project, whether it's to buy the supplies or to visit the library to get a book. Most importantly, do not work on the project yourself. As the parent, you can encourage, guide, and assist as necessary. The child should do the entire project on his own. Explain those guidelines to him and then let him do the work.

> **Show you are interested in school or school projects, but emphasize that your child must do the work, not you.**

Tip :

Middle/High:
Emphasize that schoolwork comes first and talking on the phone, playing games on the computer, and watching television are secondary. Schoolwork is his responsibility; your job is to guide him. Set up a calendar so your child can learn how to time-manage homework and term projects. Seeing a month at a glance will help him understand the time frame and then determine how much time each night he should spend on homework and reports. This will also help you both know when a major assignment is due and will help your child prepare and ease the stress for everyone. You can look at the due date, and say, "Have you started yet? Do you need any materials? Do you need to visit the library? I can help this Saturday." Get him to commit to a time and date that is convenient for both of you. Planning ahead will reduce stress and produce a better project. Discuss how, at certain times of the year, there will be more schoolwork than usual. Make the point that studying a little each night instead of squeezing it all in at the last minute not only makes doing the project easier, but increases his chances of producing good work. You may offer assistance and advice, but make it clear this is his project, not yours.

P.S.: Practice *What to Say* When They Say...

> **"Mom, this boy said that there are drugs being sold in the bathroom."**

> **"I hate reading! I'd rather watch TV or play with my friends. Why do you make me read every night?"**

"Are you sure that this information is true? Did anyone ever approach you? This is a good report and must be reported to the school immediately. Thank you for telling me. I am so proud of you for coming to me and knowing that I will do what I can to help you attend a safe school. It makes me feel good to know that we can communicate about most things."

"Because this is a very serious matter, I must tell the school principal about it immediately. I want to make sure that there are no drugs on campus."

"Reading every night is important. Books can be like a best friend, always there for you, ready to entertain you, help your imagination, teach you new information, and even increase your writing skills. Would it help if I read with you or even next to you? Let's set time aside every day for family reading time. I can catch up on my favorite book or the newspaper and you can read something that interests you. When would you like to go to the library together so we both can find books we like? We can then share and talk about them."

OR

"Reading is very important, for lots of reasons. First, the more you read, the smarter you get—and being a good reader helps you in all your other subjects. Books can be good friends, too, always there when you want to be entertained; they can take you away to other places or back in time or introduce you to famous people. I love to read, so why don't we set aside some family reading time each day when we can read together. Would you like to go to the library together so we both can find books we like? Or maybe you'd like to read some magazines about your favorite hobbies? We can talk about what we've read with each other."

Notes:

SECTION FOUR:
SPRING
It's Never Too Late –
Keep Communicating for Success

> "Get over the idea that only children should spend their time in study. Be a student as long as you have something to learn, and this will mean all your life."
>
> **Henry L. Doherty**

Snapshot #43: My Child Has Food Allergies and Could Not Participate in the Multicultural Food Festival

My child came home from school very upset. As part of her lesson, the teacher had a multicultural food festival for the class. My son couldn't participate in the feast. Every type of food offered contained wheat or a cheese product, and he is allergic to both wheat and dairy products. Thank goodness he was smart enough not to eat anything, because he knows that he can get a severe allergic reaction and become very sick. But the teacher did nothing for him. Everyone else ate and enjoyed themselves, and he was entirely left out. What should I do?

Tip:

Elementary/Middle/High: Speak to the teacher and remind her that this information is in your son's medical records. Check the medical records to make sure they are up to date. Remind your child how sick he gets if he eats the wrong food. You may also ask the teacher to let you know when pizza parties or other events are planned so you can send his special food in advance, making it easy for your son to participate in the festivities.

Parent-to-Parent Tip:

Usually special events, such as food parties, are announced to the students and their parents ahead of time. At that time, parents should remind teachers of their child's special needs. It is important to recognize that your child wants to be part of the group.

Send foods to school your child enjoys and can safely eat.

Snapshot #44:

My Child Was Shown an Inappropriate Movie in School

My child came home from school and told me about a movie they watched at a school party. I knew the movie and had made the decision not to allow my child to view it, even with us as a family. I called the local movie rental store, and they confirmed that it is definitely a PG-13 rated movie. What should I do?

Tip:

Elementary/Middle/High:
Call the school and voice your concern to the administration. They may not be aware that the teacher did this. Let them take care of it, but ask that they get back to you with a report on the outcome of that meeting. Also ask what the school policy is on this kind of material being shown to young students and how that policy is enforced. Request a follow-up meeting or communication so you know this will not occur again. Know school policy on movies and books. Familiarize yourself with all school policies as stated in the school's *Parent-Student Handbook*.

www.school-talk.com

Snapshot #45:

The Teacher Was Not Fair in Grading My Child's Project

My child asked for my help with his social studies project. I helped with the drawings, the three-dimensional Viking ship, and the report. The teacher gave him a B, which I just don't understand. I think it was definitely A work, especially since I am an architect by trade, and I know the ship I drew was an exact replica. What should I do?

Rubric

A rubric is a guide that tells parents and students exactly how a paper or a project will be graded. It is a detailed report that lists all the components needed to obtain a certain grade.

Tip :

Elementary/Middle/High:
Projects offer a great opportunity to spend time with your child, assisting him in researching, planning, and getting supplies. But remember, the teacher is grading your son's work, not yours. When a teacher realizes a parent put in work on a project, she may ask the child to redo some parts or take points off the rubric because she knows it is not the student's work.

Your role is to serve as a guide to your child, if needed. Make sure the project is complete and handed in on time. Be there if your child needs some assistance, but he must learn how to complete all the parts of a rubric himself and to do his very best so that he earns the grade. If the child did his own work, and you feel he did not receive a fair grade, by all means request a conference with the teacher. Ask her how your child's project was graded. The teacher should show you documentation. You may request to see an A+ project so you can compare that work to your son's. This type of feedback is helpful in setting a standard for your child's next project.

> *Be a facilitator—not the doer—of your child's projects.*

Snapshot #46:
My Child Is Being Retained

My younger child is failing and having a difficult time doing classwork. When I work with him at home, I notice the skills he learned the day before are completely forgotten. It takes him a long time to complete any written work, while my other child breezes through his work and has lots of time to play outside. I have just received a letter from his teacher that he may be retained. I'm worried that he won't pass this year, and have noticed that his self-esteem is diminishing. What should I do?

Tip :

Elementary:
Call for a conference. Hopefully, this is not the first notice you have received that your child is failing. If it is, question the teacher as to why you have never been contacted before. If you feel that the teacher has failed to communicate the risk of failing to you in a timely fashion, you may want to go to an administrator. Check past grade reports to see if there is a history of your child's being below grade level. Listen to what the teacher has to say, and then ask for advice on how to proceed. Ask the teacher for specifics on what you can do at home to help him, as well as what the school is doing. If your child will definitely be retained, ask that the school give you the district and school guidelines for retention. Many schools have procedures they must follow to retain a child. Recommend that the school develop strategies to help him succeed. If, by a certain date, your child is not progressing with the strategies in place, request that he be tested for a learning disability. Your child may need to develop procedures and routines as well as effective study techniques and habits to ensure his success. Work with the school and put a plan in place that can be followed at school as well as at home. Make sure you get a copy of all the conferences, with signatures of all present. Keep a record and start a log. Set a timeline for the upcoming school year. You may also want to request that your child have a different teacher the following year if, in fact, he is being retained. You are your child's biggest advocate.

Middle/High:
Talk to the guidance counselor to find out what courses or credit hours your child needs to complete to be promoted to the next grade. Next, meet with all of his teachers. Find out how he is doing and ask their opinion on whether he will be promoted or retained this year and how many classes or courses he is failing. Call the child into this conference so he knows exactly what is expected of him in both his schoolwork and classroom behavior. He may surprise you and tell you he feels he can't make it on his own and either ask for a tutor or a support system to help him succeed. You may also want to ask the school to test your child for a learning disability. Work with the school counselor and the teachers and come up with a plan. Some high schools will promote a child to the next grade level if they retake the class that they have failed as an elective, take it as a night class, or even take it on the Internet, if available.

Snapshot #47:

My Child Broke His Leg and the School Never Called Me

I am furious. My son tripped at school during recess and injured his leg. Even though he told the teacher that it hurt, she said it was probably nothing. When I picked him up from school, he was limping badly. I decided to take him to the doctor and when they took X-rays, they found he had a hairline fracture to his ankle. How can anyone be so insensitive? I am extremely angry, especially since no one called me. I never received any notification of an accident report. What should I do?

Tip:

Elementary/Middle/High:
Contact the school immediately and schedule a meeting with the school principal and the teacher who was in charge at the time your child got hurt. Get the facts. Listen to their side of the story and try to see where the breakdown in communication took place. Make sure that the school establishes or follows procedures so that this never happens again. Any child who becomes injured should report to the office immediately. An accident report should be filled out and the parent notified.

It is important that your child know when it is necessary to let an adult know he needs help and immediate attention.

Parent-to-Parent Tip:

You may want to discuss with your child how to emphasize to a teacher that something really hurts and that he would feel more comfortable if his mother came and picked him up.

Snapshot #48:

The School Is Always Asking for Money

Every time I turn around, the school is asking for money. There are field trips, fundraisers, and bake sales. Now it's the end of the year and graduation is here. They want money for an expensive senior trip, the cap and gown, a graduates' dance, and a present for the teacher. I don't even like the teacher—why should I buy her a present? I can't keep dishing out money. I thought this was a public school, not a private school. On the other hand, I don't want to disappoint my child. All of these things are important to her. What should I do?

Tip:

Elementary:

Call the school and ask to speak to the guidance counselor or staff member who may be able to assist you with your problem. There is always someone who will listen with a sympathetic ear. Explain that this additional financial obligation is difficult for you, but you don't want your child left out of any of the activities. You could offer your time and services to help with some of the organization of these programs. You may also suggest that some of the money that's come in through school fundraisers be earmarked as scholarships for students who can't afford some of the end-of-school activities. If you approach the meeting with a calm attitude and offer some workable ideas, a solution that works for everyone can usually be found.

Middle/High:

Suggest having the child get a part-time job or do chores for neighbors to earn extra money for the senior trip. The school can also try and get a sponsor to donate money for students who are unable to afford to go. At a parent meeting, you may express the need for a fundraiser that the children run and organize, like a car wash, where all the money raised will be earmarked to offset the cost of the trip.

Parent-to-Parent Tip:

Many times schools have money set aside for special activities and events for students who may otherwise be unable to participate due to financial reasons. If you have a financial hardship, you may want to inquire if this is the case in your child's school.

Snapshot #49:

I Am Concerned About Adult Supervision at the End-of-the-Year Dance

In the car the other day with my daughter and her friends, I heard them discussing the end-of-the-year dance. They giggled when they talked about "close dancing," who is going with whom, whether their moms would let them use makeup, and what they were going to wear. At first I didn't think I needed to worry about any of this innocent talk. Then I realized there was a bigger picture: Who would be attending the dance? What food and drinks would be served? Who would be supervising? What would the kids want to do afterwards? What should I do?

Tips to follow for the school dance:

1. Call the school to find out the details: time, location, and who are the adults in charge.
2. Talk to your child about the behavior you expect.
3. Offer to be a chaperone.
4. Form a carpool.
5. Make sure you are near a phone so your child can reach you at any time during the evening.

Tip:

Elementary:
Call the school and ask who will be coordinating this event. If you are satisfied that there will be enough chaperones and off-duty police monitoring the parking lot, then have a talk with your daughter on how you expect her to behave no matter what the other classmates are doing. This is the time to revisit your discussions about the values you have tried to instill and the behavior you expect. Make it clear that if she runs into a difficult situation, she should call you and you will be right there. Be near a phone that evening so she can reach you if she needs to. You may also want to sign up to be one of the chaperones at the event.

Middle/High:
Contact the school and make sure there will be enough chaperones and off-duty officers at the event to make you feel comfortable sending your daughter. Discuss all possible scenarios with her and explain you are just a phone call away. Don't be naïve about what kids might do these days. Statistics show that boy-girl relationships are starting at younger ages than ever before. You may want to offer to chaperone or assist in the preparation of the event. Check with your teenager on this one. She may not want you there. It might be embarrassing in front of her friends. The more input, the better and safer the dance will be.

Snapshot #50:

The Summer Break Is Too Long and My Child Will Forget All She Has Learned

I am worried my child will not keep up with the skills she has learned and will lag behind when she starts the next grade. I want her to get good grades and don't feel that she will be ready unless she does something academic over the summer session. What should I do?

> **Be an advocate for year-round learning and for summertime reading and math family time.**

Tip :

Elementary:

Before the school year is over, have a meeting with your child's teacher or the administration and express your concerns. Request a list of skills expected of students for the upcoming year, the curriculum goals for the class, and a summer reading list. Inquire about any books or novels the teacher can recommend or activities that would help maintain your child's present skill level. You may also want to ask if there are any commercial products or programs that would keep your child entertained while increasing her skills so she will be ready to go forward on the first day of school.

Middle/High:

Have a team meeting with all your child's teachers and request recommendations for academic work over the summer. Also ask if there are any summer programs that mix academic review with some activities or sports. Sometimes these types of programs are found in the guidance office, at local community or city parks, and at recreation departments, libraries, or local learning institutions. The local school district may be able to answer your questions on this concern.

Parent-to-Parent Tip:

Save assignments, book reports, worksheets, and consumable books that are brought home at the end of the school year. Use these items as a review for your child during the summer. Continue to make reading a priority. Many times libraries have free programs in the summer to encourage reading. Call the local library and ask if they are having any summer programs for children. Create a family reading time each evening and also spend time on reviewing math facts or other skills learned the previous year.

Snapshot #51:
The School Wants My Child to Keep a Summer Journal

My son has an assignment to write in a journal every day over the summer break, according to the school website. The work he does in the journal will be part of his language arts grade when he returns to school. This seems like a waste of time to me. I am not sure why this has to be done, and I am too busy to check if he completes it every day. I am frustrated by this requirement, which just seems like busywork. What should I do?

Tip:

Elementary:
As the parent, it's your job to know what will be expected of him and to support him in doing his best to complete the work. One of the goals for students at your son's level might be to improve writing skills; practicing over the summer will give your son a jump start. It is important to your child's success that you support this goal. Set aside a few minutes each day to read the journal with your child; this could be just before bed or any time that fits your routine. You could even set an example by writing with him on some days. If your child is in kindergarten/first grade, you may want to write the sentences for him as he tells you what he wants to say. To help him improve his writing and handwriting skills, have him use a yellow marker or crayon to trace the words you wrote. Encourage him to try and form the letters and words after you write them.

Middle/High:
Encourage your child to follow all the summer requirements the school has assigned. Check up on his work, making sure it is being completed with care and skill. Your support and involvement are important, as your child takes his cue from you. Explain to him that this assignment will be part of his grade and that by spending just a few minutes a day writing, he can start the semester off on a positive note. Set up a daily schedule to work on the journal. Let him pick the time to write, and you pick the time to review it with him.

Parent-to-Parent Tip:

Reading and writing are connected, so you want your child to both read and write. Role-model and practice with your child by writing or e-mailing letters to friends and relatives. Get him involved too. You can also write about books that you have read, about a trip you've taken, about your pet—the possibilities are endless. These kinds of activities are not only fun, but help your child accomplish two educational goals in one: reading and writing. Try to be supportive of the school and its teachers, because children will often use their parents' criticism as an excuse for not following the rules and regulations.

Snapshot #52:

My Child Has Come Down With "Summeritis"

As the school year draws to a close and with two weeks before summer vacation, my child seems to be getting into trouble more and more. Her grades are dropping and she is becoming extremely social. The principal has had me in the office several times to discuss the recent behavior change. I am getting tired of these complaints, but what I'm really worried about is summer vacation. I need to keep her occupied and out of trouble. What should I do?

Experts agree that the more you write the better you read, and the more you read the better you write.

Summer vacation lasts a long time. Make plans for your child.

Tip:

Elementary:

Work with the teacher and the school and implement a behavior plan immediately. Just because there are two weeks left of school does not mean that your child is free to write off the remainder of the year. Sit with your child and have a talk about this lazy attitude. If you have no formal plans for summer coming, now is the time to make them. A short family trip may not be enough, especially if you are a working mom. Many communities run summer camps, and there are countless programs offered by private and public institutions. You can also look in local newspapers, which usually have a section dedicated to activities for children. Give the local city parks department a call for their program ideas. This is also the time to look for educational services, so your child can bump up her skills and be prepared to start the new academic year with a new outlook.

Middle/High:

Sit with your child and have a talk. Set up a behavior plan and some definite ground rules. Again, just because there are two weeks left of school does not allow for your child to write off the remainder of those two weeks. Arrange for you and your child to speak with your school's guidance counselor. Some schools have a policy that a child can be retained or her academic grade withheld if she slacks off at the end of the year. The school counselor may be able to offer suggestions and help you work out a summer schedule so your child is kept busy and productive. There are many opportunities for her to volunteer, attend camps, both public and private, be tutored, or work at a part-time job.

P.S.: Practice *What to Say* When They Say…

"Everybody skips class once in a while or comes to class late and their parents don't do anything about it."

"Every parent must decide what is right for his or her child. We don't follow what other parents do, but make the decision that is best for you."

"Going to school is the top priority in our family and being on time for class is just as important. These rules are important, and as your parents, we expect you to obey them."

"If you would like, we can set aside a time we can talk about some of our other rules. You should be clear about how we feel and what we expect, and you could let us hear your point of view."

"I am not going back to that school! They don't understand me. They want to keep me in the same grade next year. I won't go!"

"I think we need to set aside a time when you and I, and perhaps your teacher, can sit down with you and discuss why we have come up with this as the solution for next year. You know that your grades have not been good this semester, and while we have tried many different ways to help you learn all the new concepts, you still are having trouble learning. You just haven't done as well as we would like you to do, and the school and I think that this is the best answer to your problem. I am trying to understand how you feel and know that your friends are moving on to the next grade and you are not, but you can make new friends and your learning must come first. We will need to talk a lot more so during the year we can solve any learning problems that you may be having right away. I am here to help you achieve success and so is the school. You have to let us know when the work is getting too hard and you just are not catching on. If you don't tell us right away, we won't be able to assist you. The sooner you report your difficulty, the faster we can help."

OR

"I think we need to set aside a time when you and I, and perhaps your teacher, can sit down with you and discuss why we have come up with this as the solution for next year. You know that your grades have not been good this semester, which tells us that you aren't learning the concepts as well as you should. If you don't understand what's being taught this year, you will have a very difficult time in the next grade. You might become discouraged and frustrated and give up on school. By repeating this grade, you can become much stronger in learning what you need to know to move on."

"I know you are disappointed and wish you were moving up to the next grade with your friends, but you will make friends in your new class. Your education is extremely important and it must come first. I'd like to try a new strategy this year to make sure we solve any problems quickly. I am here to help you do well, and so is your teacher. We will do whatever we can to help you succeed. Your job is to let us know right away when the work becomes hard for you and you're having trouble catching on. The longer you wait to let us know, the more difficult it will be for you to catch up. So, tell us right away, and we can quickly solve the problem together. I know you'll do much better this year and you'll feel good about school."

Notes:

Epilogue

"Anyone who stops
learning is old,
whether at twenty
or eighty."
Henry Ford

www.school-talk.com

May you continue your journey of communicating effectively with everyone who crosses your path. The more you practice the tools and techniques provided here, the better a communicator you will become. By communicating effectively, you will not only serve your own needs, you will also be better equipped to serve those of your children and family.

We send our best wishes for your continued growth from every communication opportunity that comes your way. We would love to hear from you! How did the book help you, what were your favorite snapshots, and what tips or worksheets did you like best? Please send us your comments.

You can write to us at:

School Talk
9737 N.W. 41 Street, #356
Miami, FL 33178

We look forward to effectively Communicating with You!

Share Your Snapshots

Your Snapshot

How do you make communication easier?

We invite you to share with us your snapshots. Please let us know what situations you have dealt with, what tools you have developed, and what worksheets you use to make your communications easier. We would love to feature you in our next book.

Please send submissions to:
School-Talk
submissions@school-talk.com

You can also visit and access e-mail at the school-talk.com website at:
http://www.school-talk.com or personally e-mail Cheli and Ruth at:
Cheli at: Cheli@school-talk.com
and **Ruth at: DrRuth@school-talk.com**

We hope that you have enjoyed reading *Parent Talk!* as much as we have enjoyed writing it.

APPENDIX A
From One Parent to Another: Worksheets for Your Child's School Success

WORKSHEET #1:
Communication Skills Assessment Pretest/Posttest

Directions: Check "Y" for Yes and "N" for No to give the answer you find most appropriate.

- ☐Y ☐N 1. I am comfortable speaking with teachers.
- ☐Y ☐N 2. I listen more than I talk.
- ☐Y ☐N 3. I value teacher input.
- ☐Y ☐N 4. I like to visit my child's classroom.
- ☐Y ☐N 5. I am comfortable asking questions at school.
- ☐Y ☐N 6. I come prepared to meetings with the teacher.
- ☐Y ☐N 7. I ask for solutions and methods when I do not know the answers.
- ☐Y ☐N 8. I make time to go to shows and school presentations/expos frequently.
- ☐Y ☐N 9. I do not believe that I know more than teachers do.
- ☐Y ☐N 10. I do not mind if an administrator sits in on a conference.
- ☐Y ☐N 11. I make eye contact during teacher meetings.
- ☐Y ☐N 12. I respect the opinions of teachers and other school staff.
- ☐Y ☐N 13. I feel uncomfortable when teachers call me in for a conference.
- ☐Y ☐N 14. I smile and greet teachers.
- ☐Y ☐N 15. I initiate teacher contact immediately, as concerns arise.
- ☐Y ☐N 16. I am at ease when talking with teachers or other school staff about difficult situations.
- ☐Y ☐N 17. I communicate frequently with my child's teacher.
- ☐Y ☐N 18. I admit to the teacher that I need assistance and information.
- ☐Y ☐N 19. I am comfortable talking with teachers/principals/specialists.
- ☐Y ☐N 20. I like to have teacher talks.

Count up the number of Yes answers and then find the corresponding comments below.

If you scored 18 or higher, you are on your way to becoming an effective communicator.

If you scored 15 to 18, you may want to read carefully those chapters addressing areas in which you are weak and practice the authors' techniques. The other chapters may give you further insight and communication skills to benefit your own conversational style.

If you scored below 15, you will want to read all the chapters. Practice the techniques, asking your friends and family to assist you. When you're ready to use the techniques, you may want to start by applying them in more simple situations or by talking to those parents with whom you feel comfortable before you tackle the more difficult situations.

WORKSHEET #2:
Quarterly Self-Evaluation Checklist

Answer these questions at the end of each reporting quarter.

1. What parenting techniques am I using?
   Most often: _____
   Not enough: _____

2. What works best? _____

3. What works least? _____

4. How can I improve? _____

5. Am I assisting my child to do his best at all times? _____

6. Am I consistent with communicating routines? _____
   Place a check for Yes. If not, have suggestions on how you can improve.
   ☐ Homework   ☐ Teacher Conferences
   ☐ Discipline   ☐ E-mails
   ☐ Reading the School Newsletters   ☐ School Websites

7. Am I looking at **The Assessment Tracker** on page 29 to see if my child is improving or do I need to work with him/her more to increase his/her scores? _____
   If not, what can I do? _____

8. Am I asking for teacher assistance? _____

9. Am I checking my child's grades on the report card? _____

10. Am I setting high expectations for my child? _____

WORKSHEET #3:
Who's Who at the School
Important School Staff and Their Contact Phone Numbers

WAYS TO COMMUNICATE
Here are some of the ways to communicate with your child's school:

By Phone: Name of School: _____

Name of Principal/Assistant Principal: _____

Name of Counselor: _____

School's Phone Number: _____

School's Attendance Line: _____

By Website: School's Web Address: _____

Various E-mail Addresses: _____

_____

_____

By Mail: Name of School: _____

School's Address: _____

Via Teacher: Name of Child's Teacher: _____ Room Number: _____

Via Parent Teacher Association:

Name of Parent Association Chairperson or President: _____

Parent Association Phone Number (if different than school): _____

School District's Phone Number: _____

State Board of Education's Phone Number: _____

WORKSHEET #4:
30 Ways to Help Out Your Child's School When You Work Full-Time

1. Sharpen pencils.
2. Distribute newsletters.
3. Monitor campus during lunchtime.
4. Support school events, such as ice cream socials.
5. Send old magazines to school.
6. Donate your child's old books and toys.
7. Donate toys for playground.
8. Type up newsletters.
9. Photocopy weekly news.
10. Go through Lost and Found bin once a week.
11. Ask local businesses in your area how they can help out the schools.
12. Donate items for science experiments.
13. Donate items for class parties.
14. Be part of the fun during social events; manage a booth.
15. Consider volunteering in the school office a few hours a week.
16. Consider calling parents regarding upcoming school events.
17. Affix address labels on school's outgoing newsletters and mail.
18. Donate stamps and other school supplies.
19. Donate your office's disposable papers to school.
20. Donate a cell phone to the school. Cell phones are vital to have during emergencies.
21. Donate emergency supplies such as flashlights, batteries, blankets, and first aid items.
22. Call your child's teacher once in a while to see if he/she needs anything for the classroom.
23. Donate snacks such as juices or crackers for the school.
24. Participate in fun activities such as jog-a-thons and picnics.
25. Consider chaperoning during field trips.
26. Donate old computer games.
27. Consider helping out in editing the yearbook.
28. When walking around during school events, take pictures of other people besides your child. When the pictures are developed, donate them to the school office for the school yearbook.
29. Consider helping out in maintaining the school's website.
30. Purchase practical items that the parent-teacher organizations are selling. It is certain that proceeds will go directly to the school.

WORKSHEET #5:
Getting to Know My Child

My Child: _____

	ALWAYS	SOMETIMES	NEVER	ADDITIONAL INFORMATION
1. Reads books on his/her own?				
2. Writes in a diary or keeps a journal?				
3. Asks for homework assistance?				
4. Plays computer games frequently?				
5. Watches more than an hour of television daily?				
6. Likes to have friends come over?				
7. Participates in after-school activities (sports, clubs)?				
8. Likes to complete homework as quickly as possible?				
9. Likes to do his/her best?				
10. Likes to keep to a schedule?				
11. Completes work on time?				
12. Does reports ahead of time?				
13. Enjoys being alone?				
14. Strives to get all A's on his/her report card?				
15. Is respectful of all adults?				
16. Enjoys doing school projects?				
17. Does chores around the house without being told?				

18. My child's strengths are: _____

19. My child's weaknesses are: _____

20. Goals I would like my child to achieve throughout this school year: _____

_____

APPENDIX B
Bringing the Art of Communication to You: Workshops and Coaching Programs

PROGRAMS OFFERED BY CHELI AND RUTH:

- Let's Talk! Learning the Art of Effective Communication

- Parent Talk! Artfully Communicating With Teachers

- 30-Day Personal Coaching Program—A Communication Blueprint for Your Child's Success

A Message from Cheli & Ruth

Thank you for considering one of our breakthrough programs for your personal development. We look forward to having the opportunity to offer you a motivational, thought-provoking, fun program rich in both content and humor. Our list of clients includes parents, teachers, principals, superintendents, and others who want to become effective communicators.

Here's what we want you to know more than anything else . . .

We understand firsthand the freedom that comes with communicating effectively. Like you, we have been there. As parents we have had the in-the-trenches experiences; we have created a continuum of effective techniques thousands of individuals have used to achieve successful communication. But good communication is an ongoing exercise, and for people to continue to learn and to use the tools we offer, those tools must be easy to access. To that end, we have written the book *Parent Talk!: The Art of Effective Communication With the School and Your Child,* which we can also have available to complement our program.

Learning how to effectively communicate is a necessity. People who know how to communicate well can head off problems before they arise, build strong relationships, create partnerships, and chart a path for their children's success.

Which is a better expenditure of time, money, and effort: constantly having to remedy the problems that result from communication breakdowns, or being able to address difficult situations proactively through skilled communication? The choice is clear: Knowing how to communicate effectively is essential, and we can teach you that skill.

Our programs have been tried and tested to provide you with first-class, professional information and materials. You can choose from a wide variety of our proven courses or have us customize one for your needs.

Contact us and tell us your communication challenge. We want to help you!

Regards,
Cheli Cerra, M.Ed.
Ruth Jacoby, Ed.D.

P.S. *When you want your people to communicate effectively so that misunderstandings no longer steal time and create hard feelings, contact Cheli and Ruth for a customized, personalized, hands-on, humor-based keynote or seminar at their website, http://www.school-talk.com. The quicker you respond, the faster your staff will begin to learn how to communicate effectively.*

Let's Talk!
Learning the Art of Effective Communication

A successful communicator knows his audience and how to get his point across without creating any misunderstandings. In this hands-on, fun, and informative program, you will learn the tools necessary to begin artfully communicating with others. Learn how to:

• **Use key words to diffuse hostile situations;**
• **Listen effectively;**
• **Clearly convey your point to get your message heard; and**
• **Create positive relationships through effective communication.**

Cheli and Ruth use hands-on, personal experiences and real-life case studies to demonstrate and teach the tools necessary in learning the art of effective communication.

Book this program for your next meeting or convention and let Cheli and Ruth teach the staff within your organization the steps necessary to diffuse hostile situations, learn the art of listening, and create a positive communication-friendly environment.

Parent Talk!
Artfully Communicating With Teachers

The power of this program comes from real-life in-the-trenches solutions to common and uncommon communication problems. In this no-nonsense, hands-on program, you will leave with a practical action plan to begin effectively communicating with your child's teacher and the school. The participants will learn communication tools that will make them:

- **Proactive;**
- **Organized;**
- **A good record-keeper; and**
- **An accurate reporter of information.**

Cheli and Ruth will provide assessments, tools, and practical techniques that help participants to organize their thoughts and follow a point-by-point plan for communicating effectively. Like thousands of others who have gone through the program, you will master a proven system to achieve the art of effective communication and establish a positive working relationship with teachers.

30-Day Personal Coaching Program–A Communication Blueprint for Your Child's Success

This 30-day coaching program will help you become a strong advocate for your child in school. Embark on a journey that will teach you the best techniques and strategies to use for your child's school success. From the first self-assessment you will begin to map your own personal blueprint for educational success. Don't be left behind. Know what to do and what to say to get your voice heard and guarantee success for your child. Cheli and Ruth use situations, snapshots, and activities to personally coach you. This program is fun, educational, and informative. You will learn how to:

- **Improve your child's grades;**
- **Adjust your child's study methods to uniquely suit his or her needs;**
- **Use key phrases to capture attention with teachers;**
- **Talk effortlessly through difficult communication situations; and**
- **Learn the number-one secret to crafting success for your child in school.**

Sign up for this coaching program today and leave with your personal communication blueprint that you can begin to implement immediately.

About
the Authors

About Cheli Cerra

For more than 18 years, she has helped thousands of children achieve school and life success. As a school principal and a mother of two, Cheli knows firsthand the issues that teachers, parents, and children face. She was the founding principal of one of the first K-8 schools in Miami-Dade County, Florida, Everglades Elementary. The school of 1,500 students received an A+ rating from the Florida Department of Education for two consecutive years under Cheli's leadership.

Cheli is the founder of Eduville, Inc., a company that provides resources and strategies for parents and teachers to help their children achieve school and life success. Among her resources are Smarter Kid Secrets, a free monthly e-zine, and her website http://www.eduville.com, full of tips, techniques, and strategies useful for anyone interested in helping a child succeed. Cheli serves on the Florida Advisory Board for GreatSchools.net, a nonprofit, online guide to K-12 education.

Recognized as "The Right Choice" by *Woman's Day* magazine, and featured on over 30 radio shows throughout the country, Cheli is committed to helping teachers and parents come together for the success of children. Her seminars, coaching programs, and presentations have provided strategies that empower her audiences to action. She will captivate you by teaching the lessons learned from her in-the-trenches experience in public education. As a wife and a working mother of two, she understands the reality of everyday life and creates strategies to meet these challenges quickly and easily. Her powerful message of immigrating to this country, learning the language, and adapting to a new culture also give Cheli a unique insight to the real-world challenges children face today.

Co-creator of the School-Talk Success Series: *Teacher Talk!*, *Parent Talk!*, *School Board Talk!*, and *Principal Talk!*
For more information, go to http://www.school-talk.com.

About Dr. Ruth Jacoby

Dr. Ruth is the founding principal of the Somerset Academy charter schools, which include five charter schools with 1,250 students in prekindergarten through tenth grade. She has more than 30 years of experience as an administrator and educator, in traditional public, private, and charter schools. Under her leadership, Somerset Charter School became one of the first charter schools to receive SACS (Southern Association of Colleges and Schools) accreditation. Her middle school received an A+ rating from the Florida Department of Education in its first year of operation.

Dr. Ruth received her Ed.D. degree in Child and Youth Studies for Children from Birth through 18 Years from Nova Southeastern University, and her Master of Science in Special Needs and Bachelor of Science in Early Childhood and Elementary Education from Brooklyn College.

During the past three years, Dr. Ruth has become actively involved in educating other charter school personnel in how to develop standards-based curriculum and assessments. Her school was one of the founding partners of the Tri-County Charter School Partnership, which has implemented three South Florida Annenberg Challenge grants in student assessment and school accountability and two Florida Charter School Dissemination Grants. She serves on several governing boards for charter schools in Miami-Dade and Broward counties, Florida, and is an active member of the Florida Consortium of Charter Schools.

Co-creator of the School-Talk Success Series: *Teacher Talk!*, *Parent Talk!*, *School Board Talk!*, and *Principal Talk!* For more information, go to http://www.school-talk.com.

A Very Special Thanks To:

Our children: Alexandra, Frank, Sari, and Scott for inspiring us to write this book;
Our husbands: Tom Cerra and Marty Jacoby for their unconditional love;
Our editors: Ana Del Cerra, Vicki McCowan, and Paula Wallace for their thoroughness;
Our designer: Henry Corona for his creativity;
Our Assistant: Betty Perez for her diligence and patience; and
All of the teachers, parents, and children who have touched our
lives; and **you**, our reader, for reading, absorbing,
learning, and sharing.

"Effective communicators always leave a piece of wisdom with their audience."

To your artful and effective communication.

Cheli and Ruth

Let us hear from you... send us your snapshots. Email Cheli and Ruth at:

Cheli Cerra
Cheli@school-talk.com

Ruth Jacoby
DrRuth@school-talk.com

The *School Talk!* Series
by Cheli Cerra, M.Ed. and Ruth Jacoby, Ed.D.

Parent Talk! The Art of Effective Communication With the School and Your Child

This must-have guide for parents provides 52 "snapshots" of just about every conceivable situation than can arise between a parent, a student, and a school and provides clear, simple suggestions for positive solutions. From "My child's friend is a bad influence" to "I don't understand the results from my child's test," it covers all the typical events in a student's school experience.

ISBN 0-471-72013-5   **Paperback**   **www.josseybass.com**

Teacher Talk! The Art of Effective Communication

"An amazing compilation of what to say to parents. This book is a must have for your professional library."

—*Harry K. Wong, Ed.D., author of the bestselling* The First Days of School

An essential guidebook for all teachers that presents effective strategies for handling 52 common situations and simple ways to communicate with students, parents, and administrators. Features worksheets, checklists, sample letters, and more.

ISBN 0-471-72014-3   **Paperback**   **www.josseybass.com**

Principal Talk! The Art of Effective Communication in Successful School Leadership

Principal Talk! provides simple communication strategies and advice to keep teachers, students, parents, staff, and the community in your corner. A must-read for today's educational leader to be successful in today's reform climate.

—*Jack Canfield, co-author,* Chicken Soup for the Teacher's Soul

This user-friendly, quick reference presents 52 "snapshots" of communication issues faced by busy principals and assistant principals in working with staff, parents, teachers, and the community.

ISBN 0-7879-7911-2   **Paperback**   **www.josseybass.com**

School Board Talk! The Art of Effective Communication

For both the aspiring and the veteran school board members, this book offers tips, worksheets, and practical advice to help board members develop and improve communication skills, survive in political office, and make a difference in education. In its user-friendly, easy-to-browse pages you'll find 50 "snapshots" and solution strategies on topics such as: casting the lone "no" vote and surviving, keeping your family in your fan club, building a school board team, handling constituent calls, and conquering the e-mail and memo mountain.

ISBN 0-7879-7912-0   **Paperback**   **www.josseybass.com**